FORTNITE

FORTNITE

THE ULTIMATE UNAUTHORIZED GUIDE

GRANT TURNER

ST. MARTIN'S GRIFFIN
NEW YORK

The editor would like to thank Zachary and Joshua,
without whom this book would not exist.

www.stmartins.com

22 MEDIAWORKS, INC.
www.22mediaworks.com
lary@22mediaworks.com
PRESIDENT: Lary Rosenblatt
DESIGN AND PRODUCTION: Fabia Wargin Design
WRITER: Grant Turner
COPY EDITOR: Laurie Lieb
Thanks Sandro

The Library of Congress Cataloging-in-Publication Data is available
upon request.

ISBN 978-1-250-31722-3 (trade paperback)
ISBN 978-1-250-31723-0 (ebook)

Our books may be purchased in bulk for promotional, educational, or
business use. Please contact your local bookseller or the Macmillan
Corporate and Premium Sales Department at 1-800-221-7945,
extension 5442, or by email at MacmillanSpecialMarkets@macmillan.com.

First Edition: July 2018

10 9 8 7 6 5 4 3 2 1

TABLE OF CONTENTS

INTRODUCTION

You've probably heard a lot about this video game called Fortnite Battle Royale and you're wondering how to play. Or maybe you've played a few times with friends and want to amp up your game to become a contender. Whether you're totally new to Fortnite or have been playing for several months, there's always something else to learn about it. And with new features released weekly, keeping up is challenging.

Fortunately, you have this book in your hands. It will guide you step by step from start to finish in installing, playing, and winning Fortnite. Granted, you won't win every time— even professional players like Ninja, Myth, Dark, and Muselk don't win all the time—but you can get better at acquiring resources and protecting yourself from elimination. With the strategies, tips, and tricks shared here, you can significantly boost your odds of staying alive longer and being well-equipped for the final battle.

One of the Most Popular Games Around

Fortnite is popular for a variety of reasons, perhaps the top one being that it's free. You can play it on your phone, your PC, or your Xbox or PlayStation 4. It's also one of the few cross-platform games, meaning you can play against friends who are on PCs or Xboxes when you're on a PlayStation 4. This versatility across platforms makes it possible for virtually anyone, anywhere, to join the fun.

The skills required to win Fortnite are also different from typical war- or battle-themed games, which rely mainly on shooting accuracy. In Fortnite, the core skill is building—building ramps to get up and away and building structures to protect yourself. The ability to shoot various guns is almost secondary. Yes, you do have to be good at shooting a gun, but you'll only have those opportunities if you can build to stay alive.

Getting Started

If you haven't already, download and install Fortnite onto your preferred gaming platform—detailed instructions are in Chapter 1. Then start playing. The only way to get experience and spot strategies for success is by jumping in, literally, and getting a feel for the terrain, the obstacles, and how to maneuver your character once on the island.

In the coming chapters you'll learn more about the best strategies for starting your game—essentially where to land—and what to do as soon as you're on the ground. Hint: It isn't to hide. Finding resources—some on the ground ready to be picked up and some stashed in chests hidden in various spots around the island—will be your first priority.

Protecting yourself from other players who are trying to eliminate you is your next challenge. The only way to win Fortnite Battle Royale is to be the last player standing. That means you'll want to learn more about landing, looting, and protecting yourself—all of which are covered in detail here.

Sure, the first few times you play you're likely to be one of the first players eliminated. That's okay. You have to start somewhere. But over time, by applying what you learn here, you'll discover you can outlast many other players and maybe even get some wins under your belt.

Good luck! Maybe we'll have the chance to play against each other soon.

GETTING STARTED

CHAPTER 1

How to Install Fortnite

Do you want to get in on the new gaming craze that everyone is talking about? Your first step is getting your hands on Fortnite Battle Royale. Whether you have a PC, PlayStation, Xbox, or iPhone, here are the steps you need to follow to download the free game onto your preferred platform.

PC (Mac & Windows)

If your intent is to play on your desktop or laptop computer, you first need to be connected to the Internet. Downloading the game requires a connection.

Next, open your web browser and go to https://www.epicgames.com. Once at the website, create an account by clicking the head-shaped icon at the top right. Jot down or print out all the log-in details you used so you can gain access again.

Make sure you choose Fortnite Battle Royale, which is free. Fortnite Save the World will cost you money.

Once you have successfully registered an account at the Epic Games website, download the Epic Games launcher by clicking the yellow Get Epic Games button at the top right of the page.

The yellow button you need to click is in the top right corner of the page, right next to the head-shaped icon you clicked in order to create your account.

Install the Epic Games launcher by running the file you just downloaded. When it is finished installing, open the Epic

Games launcher. You'll be asked to sign in using the log-in credentials you used when signing up.

Fill in your email and chosen password and hit the Sign In button.

Once in the Epic Games launcher, find the Fortnite Battle Royale tab along the top bar and hit Install to begin downloading the game.

In the Epic Games launcher you've just opened, there are tabs at the top that allow you to access different Epic Games titles. Click the one that says Fortnite and then click the green Install button. Once you've done this, you will be able to see your download speeds.

After the installation is complete, the download bar that appeared over the Install button will disappear and the button will now read Launch. Hit Launch, hop into battle with your friends or by yourself, and begin working your way toward that oh-so-satisfying #1 Victory Royale.

When you arrive at this menu, you are ready to play. If you are having trouble finding your way here, please review the steps to ensure that you followed them correctly.

PlayStation 4

To play, you first need to own a PlayStation 4, of course, and confirm that it is connected to the Internet.

Sign in to PlayStation Network. If you don't already have a PlayStation Network account, follow the steps on the console to set one up.

Next, open up the PlayStation Store.

This is the very first screen you are greeted with when turning on your PlayStation 4. The PlayStation Store is all the way to the left of the available options. Use your analog sticks on your controller to navigate to it.

At the top of the PlayStation Store you will see the Search button. Click on it and search for Fortnite Battle Royale.

Next, click on Fortnite and begin to download it by clicking the Download button under the title of the game.

⌃ **Click the Download button at the bottom left to add Fortnite Battle Royale to your PlayStation 4 list of games.**

When the download is complete, make your way back to your games, and open Fortnite.

Once you're in the game, you will be asked if you would like to "Sign Up" or "Log In" or "No Thanks." Select "Sign Up" if you do not already have an Epic Games account; then follow the steps. Select "Log In" if you already have an account. Then sign in. Doing this will make cross-platform play possible—meaning you can play with friends who are playing on their PC, Xbox, or mobile phone.

Now you are ready to play. Hop into battle with your friends or by yourself, and begin becoming familiar with the battlefield and all the tools and resources at your disposal.

Xbox

Make sure your Xbox One is connected to the Internet before you start to download the game.

Then sign into Xbox Live. If you don't already have an Xbox Live account, follow the steps on the screen to set one up. This will give you access to games that are available in the Xbox store.

Next, go to the Store tab on the home screen.

◀ This is the Store tab on an Xbox One console—the green button at the upper right. Find your way here.

In the Store, you will see the Search button at the top of the screen, under the featured items. Click on it and search for Fortnite Battle Royale.

❯ Once in the Xbox Store, look for the Search button near the top of the screen.

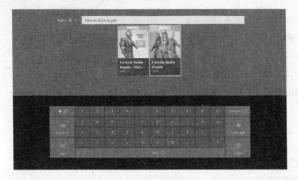

▲ Type "Fortnite Battle Royale" into the search bar and an icon should appear below it.

Click on the Fortnite button and begin to download the game by clicking the Get button under the title of the game.

▲ Although the image above says "Install," your green button will say "Get." Don't worry about this difference in appearance. Select the Get button to download the game.

When the download is complete, go back to the screen labeled "My Games & Apps" and open Fortnite Battle Royale.

Once you're in the game, you will be asked if you would like to "Sign Up" or "Log In" or "No Thanks." Select "Sign Up" if you do not already have an Epic Games account; then follow the steps. Select "Log In" if you already have an account. Then sign in. Doing this will make cross-platform play possible—meaning you can play with friends who are using other types of devices.

Once your Fortnite game is open, you're ready to start playing.

Mobile (iOS)

On March 20, 2018, Epic Games rolled out a mobile (iOS) version of Fortnite Battle Royale that can be downloaded from the App Store on any mobile Apple device newer than the iPhone 7.

CHAPTER 2

How the Game Is Played

Be the last person alive in the game—that's your goal in Fortnite Battle Royale. You start with 100 solo players (or 50 teams of two or 25 squads of four), who all land on an island simultaneously. Then it's a fight to the death as all the players work to protect themselves and gather resources that will keep them alive longer in the game.

Staying alive is the first priority of the game; good players live longer, while newer players still trying to figure out how things work are often the first to get killed off. Skilled Fortnite players who have already mastered how to stay alive in the game frequently turn their attention to maximizing eliminations as a secondary challenge—to make the game more interesting. New players who have more to learn typically hide and stay away from combat early on in order to survive and win the game. Whether you're skilled or new to Fortnite, you have to know how to use your loot to maximize the odds of staying alive.

Although Fortnite isn't the first game to adopt the Battle Royale game mode, it certainly is the first to incorporate a building technique into the action; you can build structures to get around more easily within the game. It is also the first game to provide a cross-platform experience with the purpose of bringing more players together. Unlike traditional games, Fortnite's blend of order and chaos makes every game a new experience, even for advanced players. That's why Epic Games has reached over 45 million players and has 3 million concurrent players with Fortnite.

The basic cycle of any Battle Royale game is land, loot, move, survive. However, every Battle Royale game is a little different. Luckily, Fortnite has its own perspective and game model. It's also free—a big bonus.

How the Game Begins

At the start of every game of Fortnite, all the players board a Battle Bus—a flying blue one—and skydive into the play area—the island. Up to 100 players fit on one bus—that's how many people can play in one game at one time.

Before the game officially starts, all players are in a pregame lobby and can see the path the bus will take over the island, which looks like a big map. Being able to see where the bus will travel helps you plan where you'll want to jump out and land. Beginning players will generally want to land in an unpopulated area that is safer (meaning a lower chance of being shot by others in the area). Meanwhile, more advanced players want to land where there is a maximum number of players, in order to immediately start eliminating the opposition.

The time between the moment players appear (also referred to as spawning) on the bus to the moment they touch down on the island is roughly a minute. This approach is very similar to the beginning of PlayerUnknown's Battlegrounds, another Battle Royale–style game where players start by flying into the play area on a cargo plane.

▲ The first moment spent in the game is on this Battle Bus that is traveling to the island. All players start by parachuting out of this bus.

The flight path of the flying bus changes with every game, which is important to know because it means players can't plan to go to the exact same location in every single game. It is very unlikely that a large number of players will be able to land at the same single location along the outside perimeter of the island in every game because sometimes the bus's path will be too far away from the desired location for players to head there first. To keep things interesting, some aspects of the game are randomized, including the bus path, the safe zone locations, and the locations of loot chests.

Once on the bus, players first strategize where on the map they want to land. This decision is important because the first goal is to maximize your chance of safely obtaining loot. While on the bus, you can choose when to jump off at any point. In Xbox One hit A, in PlayStation 4 hit X, and in the PC version hit the space bar when you're ready to exit the bus.

The only problem that can arise when you're parachuting out of the bus is that you end up landing in an area that is already populated with other players, who are immediately going to shoot at you. Your objective is to land and get to a loot chest as quickly as possible.

▲ This is what you see as you're gliding from the bus to the ground. You have no supplies except a pickaxe at your disposal.

Immediately after touching down on the island, your first task is to find the nearest loot chest. These chests, which are usually inside buildings, are golden boxes you need to locate and open. Loot includes items such as weapons, medical kits, and launch pads that can be used to help you outlive all the other players and teams in the game. New tools that can be used to increase the odds of winning the game are being released weekly.

When landing, you want to choose a location that will put you near as much loot as possible right from the start. This generally means that you'll want to target a well-populated area. The downside of this approach is that you'll immediately encounter other players and will have to fight them to claim the loot. Chests are located all over the island, from the attics of houses to the depths of caves. Fortunately, you can see a clue that you're near a chest—when you approach a building or area where a chest is located, you'll see a yellow glow around the box.

⌃ This is what a loot chest looks like—bathed in glowing yellow light.

Looting your chest takes just a second before the randomly selected items pop out. Along with the weapon usually come some ammunition and a small amount of building materials, either wood, brick, or metal. The main thing to remember is that all the other players in the game are landing at the same time and there's a pretty good chance that you and another player may be aiming to land near the same chest. So you need to loot as fast as you can by opening as many chests as possible.

As you move around on the island, you can check your progress in the game by looking at three different indicators in the top right corner of your screen, just under your mini-map. These include a timer and two numbers. These represent the time in minutes and seconds that have elapsed in the game—the longer you're alive, the better, obviously—the number of people still in the game, and the number of players you've personally killed.

What to Do Once You're on the Ground

After you've landed, you should be focused on trying to find loot in chests, picking up resources that are lying around (such as medical supplies, less powerful weapons, and ammunition), and shooting other players to get them out of the game and protect yourself.

You move around the island by using the W, A, S, and D keys on your PC or by using the left analog stick on Xbox One and PlayStation 4. They allow you to walk or run; to jump, use the space bar. These are the default settings that you can change later. In order to run slightly faster, hold down the Shift key on your PC and press down on your analog stick if playing on a console. Doing this will make your character sprint and you will be able to move around the map much quicker.

❯ When you open a chest, the items inside appear. This blue shield potion was found in the chest here.

When to Move Out of the Area

Once you touch down on the map, it's important to be aware of the storm. The storm covers the safe zone and moves every few minutes, covering a larger and larger area of the island and reducing the size of the safe zone. You can watch the storm countdown clock on-screen to alert you when the size of the safe zone is about to shrink. You want to get inside the safe zone and stay there, so you need to pay attention to where its boundaries are located and how much time you have to get to it. That means you may need to move as the safe zone continues to shrink.

There is an icon under the mini-map with a timer directly to the right of it—this gauge keeps track of the safe zone. If the icon depicts a storm cloud with a lightning bolt, that means it is the beginning of the game and the storm is currently not moving. As long as you have landed inside the white circle on your map, that's good. The timer next to the icon is counting down to when the storm will begin moving. If the icon shows a storm cloud moving to the right, without a lightning bolt, that means the storm is currently moving; the timer will be counting down to when the storm will stop moving. If the icon shows a blue clock, that means the timer is counting down to when the storm will begin moving again.

If you get caught in the storm, you will experience a visibility impairment that imitates an actual storm. This impairment makes it harder for opposing players within the storm to see each other. It will go away once you exit the storm.

How Do I Find Out Where I Should Go Next?

The mini-map in the top right corner of your screen shows the progression of the safe zone. The safe zone gets smaller and smaller throughout the game, so it's important to know where you need to be in order to stay safe after every wave or storm cycle. If you are outside the safe zone, you will take damage from the storm and your health will go down, which will weaken you until you get into the safe zone. At the beginning of the game, the damage from being outside the safe zone will be very small, but as the game continues the amount of damage experienced will increase. You can die if you don't get to the safe zone quickly, and if you find that you're far away from the safe zone's perimeter, because you haven't been watching your mini-map, you may not be able to survive long enough to get back into the safe zone.

In order to find out where to go before the safe zone starts to move, look at your large map. Press Tab or M if you're playing the PC version, Back on Xbox One, or Menu on PlayStation 4. As you look at the map, you'll see a white circle; this is the next location of the safe zone. If you're located outside the white circle, there will be a white line that reveals the shortest path to the safe zone. In order to stay alive throughout the game, you need to stay within the safe zone.

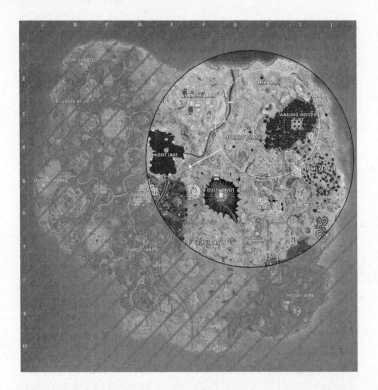

The dark shaded area surrounding the larger circle in this screenshot is the storm—you don't want to be here. The larger circle is the safe zone, which is compressing to the size of the smaller interior circle. That's where you need to be when time runs out.

What Should I Do If I Get Caught in the Storm?

If you were unable to make it to the next safe zone in time so you got caught in the storm, follow the dark blue line on your mini-map. This is the shortest path to the edge of the storm. Once you are out of the storm, your first instinct should be to heal yourself using med kits and bandages as much as you can. To make use of either one, press on the number corresponding to the box (called slots) that your bandages are located in. If your bandages are in box five, press 5 on your keyboard. Other players who were also caught in the storm may be near you, and once they are able to see you they will try to eliminate you. If you have healed and there are no other players around you, shift your focus to making it into the white circle so that you don't get caught in the storm again.

How Do I Know How Many Players I've Eliminated?

While you're moving around on the island in search of loot in chests, you also need to keep an eye out for other players. They will try to harm you, so you always need to be on the offensive, ready to shoot them when you see them. When you do successfully eliminate them, you will reduce your competition and obtain any leftover ammunition they had. If you've run out of ammunition that you collected while moving around, this is an important resource to gather.

You'll notice that as you shoot players, the number of competitors still in the game will be reduced by one. You can see the total number of players you have eliminated by checking the number to the right of the skull icon in the top right corner of your monitor, below your mini-map. Generally, the number of players eliminated from the game is largest at the very beginning and starts to taper off toward the end, as the safe zone shrinks. Those who are left are typically the more advanced competitors.

The core goal of Fortnite Battle Royale is to eliminate all the other players. It's the essence of the game. Other features, like looting and moving, are important only because they help you stay alive and provide tools for eliminating other players. Always keep in mind that there can be only one victor, so if you see any other players, you need to try to eliminate them. Of course, they will try to eliminate you at the same time, so duck.

Eliminating other players can be very challenging for beginners and takes a lot of time to master, so don't get discouraged. You have to learn how to use the weapons (mainly guns and an axe), how to build ramps that take you up higher for a better vantage point, and how to keep track of several other variables that often dictate life or death.

How Do I Know How Many Players Are Left in My Game?

During your journey to the top of the Fortnite Battle Royale scoreboard, you'll want to keep track of how many players are left in your game. Every game starts with 100 players. You can see how many are left by looking under your mini-map in the top right corner of your screen. Look for the person icon between the skull and the purple cloud. It counts down as players are eliminated. When just you and one other player are left, you'll see a number 2, and 1 after you have won the game.

Players will often get confused when they see the number 2 because they think that means there are two more players left to eliminate. But the 2 actually means there are only two players left in the game—you and one last opponent! So eliminate one more player and you've won!

How the Game Ends

❯ If you are shot at by another player and hit badly enough that you're killed, you'll receive a big notice on-screen to that effect.

If another player eliminates you, you can simply start a new game and apply what you just learned from your last one. The typical game lasts around 20 minutes, but can go as short as 10 minutes or as long as 25 or so, at which point there is no safe zone left.

The best thing about Fortnite is that it takes only a few games to learn the basics. You can go from not knowing anything about the game to getting a kill within a matter of hours. In other games that's nearly impossible to do. Here you have a chance.

If you have survived long enough and all other players in the game have been eliminated, the message "Victory Royale" will appear on your screen.

Congratulations!

CHAPTER 3

Different Modes of Play

E very game of Fortnite is different because there are several different means by which each player can acquire weapons, materials, and utilities that will maximize the chances of winning the game. At the very start of each game, when players exit the Battle Bus and skydive toward the ground, they first have to choose where they want to land. That choice is based on where they believe they can get the best weapons before anyone else, thus giving them a better chance of staying alive while the game is at its most chaotic—in the beginning, when as many as 100 players are getting off that bus.

There are four ways players can acquire weapons: "looting" from the ground, from chests, from airdrops, or from vending machines.

Ground Loot

One of the most common places to find loot in any named location, like Pleasant Park, for example, is on the ground. Most loot is located inside houses and buildings, so those are the very first places you should look.

Other weapons are just lying out in the open and available to be picked up. Players able to land onto ground loot, like weapons, at the beginning of the game are usually the first to get kills and thus also the most fully armed and ready for battle.

Players need to know that tactical and pump shotguns only spawn—that is, appear—on the ground and in vending machines. This is important because shotguns are debatably the most crucial weapon to have at the start of every game of Fortnite, when everyone only has 100 health and very few have shields that deter bullets. Thus, a weapon like a shotgun that can do high amounts of damage at close range is optimal to use when most of the players are still alive. Luckily, tactical and pump shotguns are fairly common, so they aren't difficult to find. However, if you don't acquire a shotgun within 30 seconds of landing on the ground, there is a big chance that you will be eliminated.

Other loot, such as sniper rifles, assault rifles, and all other forms of weapons or materials in the game, can also be found on the ground, but less frequently than the shotguns. Overall, ground loot is helpful, but you should still always be on the lookout for glowing chests and airdrops.

Chests

The best way to consistently get loot is by searching for chests. Chests spawn in various locations on the island. It is possible for a chest to spawn at any of the provided locations, but whether or not a chest is in the location is entirely random. You could aim to land at one chest in every single game you play but the chest may be located there only 50 percent of the time. This element of randomness is supposed to make every game of Fortnite feel different, so that no player has a guaranteed advantage right at the start of the game.

Every chest in Fortnite will give players a weapon, an extra round of the ammo for that gun, between 10 and 30 wood, brick, or metal resources for building, and sometimes a healing item. If a chest hasn't been opened, it will glow yellow, appear closed, and make an audible tone when players are around it, so keep your ears open. When a player opens a chest, the items within it fly out toward the player and onto the ground, and it loses its glow. Make sure that you don't go running to chests that have already been opened.

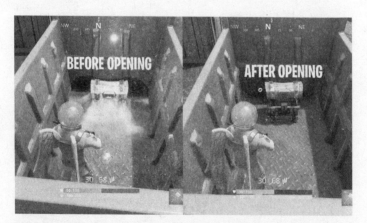

⏺ Knowing whether or not a chest has been opened is vital in the game of Fortnite. Chests are often hidden away in hard-to-reach places in order to confuse players who can hear them humming but can't see them.

Chest Locations

Chests move from game to game; however, there is a finite number of possible locations where a chest may be. With the help of Jeremy Pedron (aka "squatingdog"), we have created maps of the possible locations where chests can appear in the most popular areas of the game.

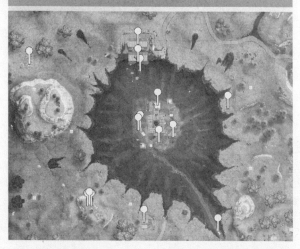

DUSTY DIVOT
CHEST LOCATIONS

FATAL FIELDS
CHEST LOCATIONS

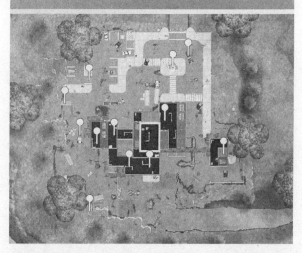

HAUNTED HILLS
CHEST LOCATIONS

JUNK JUNCTION
CHEST LOCATIONS

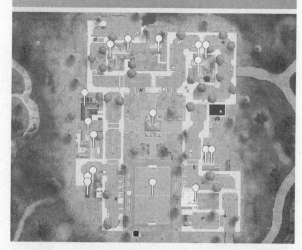

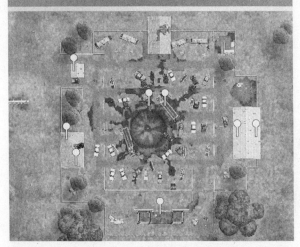

RISKY REELS
CHEST LOCATIONS

SALTY SPRINGS
CHEST LOCATIONS

SHIFTY SHAFTS
CHEST LOCATIONS

SNOBBY SHORES
CHEST LOCATIONS

TILTED TOWERS
CHEST LOCATIONS

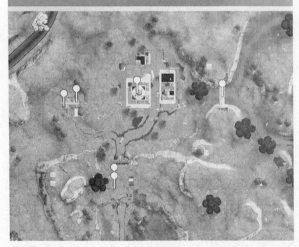

TOMATO TOWN
CHEST LOCATIONS

Llama Piñatas

One of the unique features in the game is loot piñatas, each shaped like a llama. Finding a loot piñata is extremely rare because only three spawn onto the island in each game. Also, the piñatas can appear anywhere on the map—the location is completely random every time.

Inside each piñata you are guaranteed to find 500 wood, 500 brick, and 500 metal resources, as well as a large amount of ammunition of any type and various healing items. Finding a loot llama will give you a large advantage over most players because of your surplus of building materials, full health and shields, and extra ammunition such as rockets. Always keep your eyes open for loot llamas and open them whenever possible.

⬣ **Loot llamas are extremely difficult to find in the game. If you stumble across one, you are very lucky.**

Airdrops

As your game of Fortnite plays out, you will see multiple crates slowly fall from the sky. These crates are tied to balloons that can be shot and destroyed so that the crate falls more quickly to the ground.

Inside each airdrop is usually a legendary weapon of some kind as well as a large amount of ammunition and some healing supplies. If you are able to secure an airdrop, make sure you open it right away in order to increase the deadliness of your arsenal. Stay aware of other players who are also attempting to capture the airdrop; they will kill you for the loot whenever possible.

⬆ **Airdrops fall at a slow rate that gives you, or you and your team, if you're playing with a group, plenty of time to secure the drop zone.**

Because every airdrop can be seen in the sky from almost any point on the ground, players will often debate whether battling over an airdrop that is far away is worth the risk. One tip for pointing out airdrops to your teammates, or keeping track of an airdrop as it falls from the sky, is to shoot the balloon of the airdrop. The airdrop will then display how much health it has left before the balloon can break and the crate can fall to the ground. It's relatively difficult to destroy the balloon quickly without giving away your position because of the noise your gun makes, so make sure going after a crate is worth it. If you have a good assault rifle, shotgun, and some healing items, the chances are that you won't need to chase down a supply drop for good loot. However, if a supply drop is falling very close to you, it may be a good idea to wait for it to fall to the ground so as not to give away your position.

In order to know where an airdrop is going to land on the ground, look for a trail of blue smoke and a target on the ground where the smoke lies. This marker tells you exactly where the crate will land, which is where you can then open it to get all the loot inside.

▲ When you are competing with other players who also seek to obtain the airdrop, knowing where the crate will land allows you to build your base so that the crate lands within your reach.

Vending Machines

The final way to acquire loot is to get it through the use of vending machines that allow you to purchase weapons in exchange for building materials in your possession. Vending machines spawn randomly at various locations that can be found on the map provided. Each vending machine has a color that represents the rarity of the items within it. For example, a blue vending machine will give rare items, and a gold vending machine will give legendary items. Accordingly, gold vending machines are the rarest to find and the items within them cost more than the items in other vending machines—500 materials, to be exact. In order to use the vending machine, you have to spend the building materials you have with you. Each vending machine has three different item choices: one choice for each material. You can buy an item only if you have enough materials to pay for it.

Materials RARITY	Wood	Brick	Metal
LEGENDARY	500	500	500
EPIC	400	400	400
RARE	300	300	300
UNCOMMON	200	200	200
COMMON	100	100	100

⏶ Vending machines are extremely useful when you or your teammates are not as equipped for battle as you would like to be.

Vending machines can sometimes be a gamble for players because they're forced to choose between weaponry and building. The vending machines also emphasize how helpful opening loot llamas is because the llamas provide a lot of extra building materials that you are able to gather without having to use your pickaxe. You can then exchange those extra materials for the weapons in the vending machines.

Looting is the primary way players acquire needed resources to win Fortnite, so becoming familiar with the various sources of weaponry, from a vending machine to a chest to a loot llama, can give you a serious advantage in the game.

GAME MECHANICS

CHAPTER 4

Building

Fortnite wouldn't be the same game without its unique building feature. At any point on their quest for a Victory Royale, players can use walls, floors, ramps, and pyramids for several purposes. These are the four main structures that can be built and then later modified or edited. Mastering the building feature will help you gain an advantage over other competitors by both protecting and defending you and, offensively, by positioning you for a better vantage point in eliminating other players.

Using resources you'll gather, you can build walls, ramps, floors, and pyramids out of wood, metal, and brick. Once constructed, you can then edit those structures, adding openings such as doors and windows. On ramps, you can change the orientation or make them skinnier, while pyramids have a complex set of possible changes, including turning them into a ramp or a trench for cover.

How Do You Start Building?

In order to be able to build anything, you need materials—namely, wood, brick, and metal. Each of these materials has a different health value, which reflects how strong it is. Anything you can break down with a pickaxe has a health value. For example, structures made of the strongest material, metal, provide between 74 and 370 health points. Structures made of brick, which is not quite as strong, provide 84 to 280, while structures made of wood, the weakest material, provide only 95 to 190 health points. The health points vary based on the type of structure built. This means that when enemies are shooting at your base, it will take longer for them to destroy it if you used a stronger material than if you used a weaker material.

Be careful, though, because the stronger a material is, the longer it takes for it to reach full health. Wood takes approximately 5 to 7 seconds, brick takes 10 to 15 seconds, and metal takes about 30 seconds to provide the most protection it can. If you're building quickly in order to get away or protect yourself, you're almost always going to want to choose wood, since it reaches full health the fastest. Building with metal when you need fast protection will actually work against you.

In order to collect materials for your base, you must either use your pickaxe to break down elements of the map, receive them from opening loot chests, or collect them from fallen foes. Assuming you have no materials, the quickest way to get some is by using your pickaxe. If you want wood, break down things like trees, bushes, and anything else that looks like wood. If you want brick, try knocking down some walls, roofs, and chimneys of houses. Lastly, when in search of metal, look for fences, cars, and shipping containers.

Every time you use your pickaxe to break down materials for your structures, two things will happen. First, a blue circle will appear on the object you are trying to break. Second, a notification will pop up on the left side of your screen telling

you how much of that material
you've collected. When the
blue circle appears, you
should put your crosshair
over it as you swing
your pickaxe in order
to break it down as
quickly as possible.
Not only is aiming for
the circle twice as fast,
but you also get a few
extra materials from
every hit.

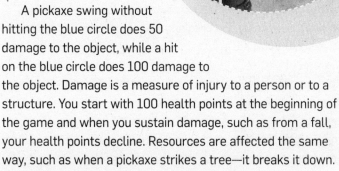

A pickaxe swing without
hitting the blue circle does 50
damage to the object, while a hit
on the blue circle does 100 damage to
the object. Damage is a measure of injury to a person or to a
structure. You start with 100 health points at the beginning of
the game and when you sustain damage, such as from a fall,
your health points decline. Resources are affected the same
way, such as when a pickaxe strikes a tree—it breaks it down.

Each time you hit the circle, you will hear a low-toned
ding and the circle will move to another location on the
object you are trying to break down—a lot like the whack-
a-mole games at amusement parks. Your goal is to hit
the circle with every swing you take so that you get the
maximum amount of materials as quickly as possible. Keep
in mind that the larger an object is, like a tree, the more
health it will have and the longer it will take to destroy with
your pickaxe; but you also get more materials than if you
were to destroy a smaller object.

⬗ The blue circle on the tree with the orange dot inside appears on any objcot you strike with your pickaxe. You must hit the object one time for the circle to appear. For striking the tree repeatedly and breaking it down, this player received 26 wood resources.

Once you have the materials you need, you can start building. First, enter building mode by pressing Q on your PC, Circle on your PlayStation, or B on Xbox. You will know you are in building mode when your player is holding a blueprint in one hand and a pencil in the other. You will also see a blue outline of the structure you have currently selected in the place where you could put it. If the outline is red, that means you can't put the structure there!

❯ As you run toward the safe zone, select your ramp option in order to get over a large hill. This image shows the blue ramp outline that appears when you are in your building mode and indicates where your object would go if you were to place it down.

After entering building mode, you will be able to scroll through five different types of structures using the scroll wheel on your PC or the left or right bumper on your gaming console. You can choose walls, floors, ramps, pyramids, and traps. Everything, with the exception of traps, costs 10 materials each to construct. It's also important to know that if you build a structure by mistake, like a wall, for example, and you then need to destroy it with your pickaxe, you will not get your materials back, so build carefully.

When Should You Build?

The best part of Fortnite's building feature is that you can use it in any and every situation. However, the two best times to build are when you are in a battle with another player and when you need to climb over something.

When in a gunfight with another player, your first instinct should always be to build first, shoot second. If you get shot at while running to the next safe zone, you should first build a wooden wall between you and the other player as quickly as possible. Use wood in that situation because it gains its health quicker than the other materials. Second, once your wall is in place, build three more walls in order to make a one-by-one box around yourself. Last, switch to your ramp-building option, jump, and place a ramp right under you facing the enemy. Once you've completed these steps, you've built your own "panic fort." It should look like this:

⬆ Panic forts are effective structures for protecting yourself from other players because they are aboveground. They also give you a slight height advantage and cover that you can use to eliminate competing players.

Another great time to build is when you are attacking an enemy fort and need cover to shield yourself from bullets while attacking. While most people would place walls in front of them (meaning they would then have to run around the walls), a better option is to use ramps. By building ramps in front of you while attacking opponents, you can quickly gain the high ground without losing your momentum.

Panic forts are especially helpful because you can build them up like towers to gain a height advantage over your opponent—that is, you can build several levels up. You can also build ramps from the top of them in order to attack your opponent by closing the distance between the two of you. Overall, when in doubt, build it out.

What Should You Build?

Depending on your situation and location, you may decide that building a panic fort made of walls and a floor or a ramp to be able to move to higher ground would be a smart move. Another smart idea is to immediately build walls between you and an enemy who starts shooting, in order to protect yourself.

Building a Wall

In order to build a wall, press F1 on your keyboard or go into editing mode on your console and scroll over to the wall structure. Walls don't have to be attached to anything else but the ground to be of use.

Building a Floor or Ceiling

In order to build a floor or a ceiling, press F2 on your keyboard or go into editing mode on your console and scroll over to the floor structure. The flat surface can be used as a floor or ceiling, depending on where you put it. If you build a wall, you have the option to add a ceiling, because the ceiling has something to attach to.

Building a Ramp

In order to build a ramp, press F3 on your keyboard or go into editing mode on your console and scroll over to the ramp structure.

Building a Pyramid

In order to build a pyramid, press F4 on your keyboard or go into editing mode on your console and scroll over to the pyramid structure.

Editing Your Structures

Sometimes, you may get trapped in your fort and need a way to escape without destroying whatever may be in your way. Luckily, Fortnite has an editing function within its building feature. Editing is, essentially, renovating your structures. The feature is extremely useful when you are in a tough situation because it can be used to outsmart your opponent.

It is important to remember that you can only edit structures that you or your teammates have built; you can't edit structures your opponent has built. To take down an opponent's structure, you'll need to shoot at it or swing at it with your pickaxe (shooting is better because you really don't want to get close enough to swing).

In order to start editing, face whatever you want to edit and press G on your keyboard if you're playing on a PC, hold Circle on a PlayStation, or hold B if playing on an Xbox. If you are playing on a console, hold the edit button down and wait for the white circle to make a full rotation around the "edit" notification on the structure you are trying to build. If you let go too soon, you will simply switch between edit mode and combat (default) mode.

Editing a Wall

Once you've built a wall, you may find it useful to add an opening, to provide either an exit or visibility, such as through a window or hole. Here are the specific steps you need to accomplish each of those modifications.

Making a Door

One of the most useful editing techniques is the ability to edit a door into your walls. To do this, simply face the wall you want to edit and hit your edit button. A three-by-three grid will appear. Select a square in the second row and then the square directly below it and press your edit button to confirm the action. If you select the center square and the square in the middle of the bottom row, once you confirm the edit a door will appear in the middle of your wall.

⏶ Press G, Circle, or B to edit your wall. This will make your wall turn into a blue three-by-three grid. Then select a middle square and one below, to form the door.

Once you press G, Circle, or B again, to confirm your edit, a door will appear in the opening you have created.

⏶ This is what a finished open door in the back of a panic fort looks like from the outside.

Lowering a Wall

In some situations you may want to be able to throw grenades at other players while maintaining the protection of a wall. By lowering it, you can throw things out of the box you're in and still remain behind a wall for protection.

⌃ Select the top three tiles of your wall while in editing mode to indicate which you want to remove to shorten your wall.

⌃ The height of your wall will be slightly higher than your player's head, which blocks your ability to see over it.

This edit is very useful when an enemy is attacking the back of your panic fort and you need to shoot your opponent while still maintaining your cover.

Making a Triangle Out of a Wall

In some situations you may need to beat a hasty exit from a panic fort and don't have the time to edit a door. Another option is to edit a triangle, essentially cutting off a corner of the wall.

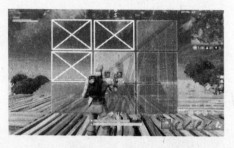

❯ Cutting off a corner of a wall can be faster than editing a door, especially when you're underneath a fort and need to get out quietly. This example of the three upper squares marked with an X shows how easy it is to cut out the top left corner of a wall, but any corner of a wall can be removed.

❮ Turning your walls into triangles is not a very useful technique during a battle with another player because it gets rid of half of the surface area of the wall you are using to protect yourself. However, if you're in a hurry and need to quickly escape through your wall without making a door, making a triangle speeds up that process because you don't have to open a door.

Taking out a triangle requires one motion to remove a corner, whereas cutting out a door requires you to wait for the door to open. The animation involved takes more time than just jumping through an opening.

Making a Window

Creating a window is helpful when the only thing that stands between you and an enemy is your wall. Instead of playing ring-around-the-rosy, chasing each other in and out of a structure, edit a window into the wall and use your shotgun to eliminate the other player.

⌃ You can make a window by selecting one of the tiles in the center row of your wall. In the picture above the center tile was chosen, but you can select any one of the three available across the center of your wall.

❯ This is what your finished window looks like.

Another option is to make both a door and a window. A window is useful for firing out of, but you can't escape through it. You can only fit through a door. There are situations when you might create a window to fire on other players and then realize you need to exit, which can only happen through a door or out from underneath by cutting out a triangle.

🔺 Many players forget that there is a way to add both a window and a door to a single wall. In the image above, the door is on the left side and the window is on the right, but they can also be switched.

▶ There are only a few occasions when you'd make both a door and a window, but the capability is there—for example,  if you've already made a window to shoot out of and find you could escape with a door. However, it's much more likely that you would just make one or the other.

Editing a Floor

Editing a floor structure is much like editing a wall: You select tiles that you want to delete in order to create an opening. If you have created a ceiling, for example, in your panic fort, by placing a floor above you, you can create an opening to escape out of the fort. Editing a floor involves only a two-by-two grid. Nonetheless, the editing technique is the same as for editing a wall.

Removing One Tile

◀ To edit your floor, click on the desired tile out of the four tiles in front of you and confirm your edit.

⬤ Removing only one tile when you edit a floor allows you to peek at opponents while you are above them. This could provide an unexpected way to attack your enemy.

Removing Two Adjacent Tiles

❯ To create this half-floor with a ramp, click two desired tiles out of the four tiles available that are touching side to side and then confirm your edit.

Removing Two Opposite Tiles

◀ In order to create a diagonal bridge-like structure when editing your floor, click two desired tiles that only touch at the corners and then confirm your edit.

⬆ This bridge can provide a way for you to peek at different enemies in opposite directions if you place it on top of your panic fort. The railings provide enough cover to make sure you don't get shot in the back.

Removing Three Tiles

◀ To create a small corner-like barricade that allows you to look down at opponents who are under you, edit your floor by clicking on three of the four available tiles and then confirm your edit.

🔺 Your end result will be a small corner about one-fourth the size of your standard floor with a small barricade to protect you as you peek at opponents below.

Editing a Ramp

The ramp structure is, in my opinion, the trickiest structure to learn how to edit. Since there are no tiles to remove or raise, the only thing you can do with the ramp is either change the angle of the incline or make it thinner in order to get out from under it. Unlike the wall-, floor-, and pyramid-editing techniques, where you click and select individual tiles, editing ramps requires you to click, hold, and drag from one area to another.

Changing the Direction of a Ramp

⬣ To effectively change the direction of your ramp, click, hold, and drag along the middle of your tiles, let go, and then confirm your edit.

⬣ Changing the direction of your ramp within a panic fort allows you to face any enemy. Always make sure your ramp is angled up toward the player you seek to destroy.

Making L-Shaped Stairs

⌃ To convert your ramps into a corner-hugging staircase, click, hold, and drag across the tiles to create an L shape and then confirm your edit.

⌃ This awkwardly shaped ramp allows you to climb to a different level within your structure. It also leaves space on the level the stairs are on so you can move around more easily and effectively in a battle scenario.

Making U-Turn Stairs

⬆ In order to complete a U-style ramp, click, hold, and drag to make a U shape with the tiles in the ramp edit and then confirm your edit.

⬆ Similar to the L-shaped ramp, this awkwardly shaped ramp allows you to climb to a different level within your structure, as well as leaving space on the level the stairs are on so you can move around more easily and effectively.

The only major difference between the U-shaped ramp and the L-shaped ramp is the shape and the direction you can travel on the stairs, so be sure to use whichever suits your situation.

Making the Ramp Thinner

⏏ To make the standard ramp thinner, click, hold, and drag along one side of the tiles.

⏏ Making your ramp thinner can be useful in combat situations when you need to retreat safely down your fort; editing the ramp is quicker than breaking down the other structures beneath you. You may need to retreat down your base if you've built too high and someone is firing explosives at you.

Editing a Pyramid

The pyramid structure is the least-used piece in the game, but that doesn't mean it's useless. There are many wacky ways players can edit the pyramid to maximize its utility. The way editing works on a pyramid is different from all the other structures. Instead of selecting a tile that you want to *vanish*, or eliminate, with the pyramid you select a tile that you want to *raise*. The pyramid has four tiles, each one representing a corner.

Raising Your Pyramid to One Corner (Ridge)

⬆ In order to raise one corner of your pyramid, click on the tile in the corner that you want raised and then confirm your edit.

◀ This pyramid edit can be useful for rounding off your bases to further fortify against enemy intrusion.

⬆ In this image you see a build utilizing this pyramid edit, which allows you to peek over two different walls at the highest possible elevation, while still being able to use the cover the walls provide. This may be seen as an upgrade to using a regular ramp as it allows you to peek at two angles instead of one.

Raising Your Pyramid to Two Adjacent Corners (Ramp)

◀ In order to raise half of your pyramid, essentially turning it into a ramp, click the adjacent two tiles you want raised and then confirm your edit.

◀ This method of editing the pyramid may seem redundant to most PC users; however, players using the other platforms the game is available on can utilize this strategy by editing their pyramids before placing them down, leaving them as your default go-to pyramid. It is easier to navigate to the pyramid than it is to navigate to the regular ramps.

Raising Your Pyramid to Three Corners (Trench)

You need two walls in order to hold a pyramid up. If the walls are not there, then the structure will collapse the moment you try to build it.

🔼 In order to edit your pyramid to raise in three corners, creating a trench-like dip in your structure, click on all but one of the four available tiles in your pyramid, creating a V shape facing outward where you want the farthest protruding tip to face, and then confirm your edit.

▶ This provides a potentially desirable way to round off a corner in your base if there are two ramps with a gap between

them, since a ramp wouldn't work as well as a corner because it would leave one side exposed.

Raising Your Pyramid to Two Opposite Corners (Wedge)

⬆ In order to construct this wedge-shaped version of the pyramid, click on two diagonal opposite tiles of the four available, and then confirm your edit.

❯ This wedge-shaped, ramp-like surface can provide a way for you to peek at opposite angles confidently since an appropriate amount of cover is available on  both sides when you're standing in its crevices.

Building can be as complex as you want it to be or as your gameplay demands. The feature is an effective way of protecting yourself when you go on the offensive or while you try to put obstacles in the way of incoming bullets. The more complicated your structures, the more advantages you can gain in the game.

CHAPTER 5

Weapons

O n your journey to win a Fortnite Battle Royale, you will need weapons. Weapons are the best way to eliminate other players.

Each weapon in the game has its own purpose and is designed to assist you in the various situations in which you may find yourself. Weapons like submachine guns, pistols, and shotguns should be used for short-range battles. Assault rifles and hunting rifles are best for medium-range shots, and scoped rifles are optimal for long-range shooting. In addition, weapons that fire explosives are extremely useful for taking out enemy bases. Not sure how to use your weapons? This chapter will provide you with all the information you need to assemble your Fortnite arsenal.

In Fortnite there are five types of ammunition: light ammunition, medium ammunition, heavy ammunition, shotgun shells, and rockets. Every gun in Fortnite requires one of these types of bullets, but each type of ammunition can be used only with specific guns. For example, light ammunition (the small bullets) is used in the minigun, submachine guns, and all of the pistols except for the revolver and hand cannon. This means that if you have a pistol, you need light ammunition in order to fire it. If you have only shotgun shells, you can't use your pistol.

⌃ To show your inventory on your PC monitor, press the letter I key to bring it up and to hide it (meaning toggle), or press the left Alt key—next to the space bar—and it will come up while the key is depressed. On the Xbox, press the View button, and on the PlayStation, press the gamepad on your controller to bring it up.

Item Rarity

Fortnite divides items within the game into different levels or tiers based on how likely or easy it is to find one. These tiers are called levels of rarity.

Weapons that are rarer are better than weapons that are less rare, and items that are rarer are much more useful. In addition, weapons of the same type, such as a pistol, also come in different levels of rarity. This means that when two of the same weapon are matched against each other, the player with the rarer weapon is more likely to win a gunfight.

There are five tiers of rarity that exist in the game. Each rarity has its own corresponding color to identify it. The lowest tier of rarity is called "common," and its corresponding color is gray. The next tier up is "uncommon," which has a green corresponding color. In the middle there is "rare," which is blue. The second best tier is called "epic," and epic items are purple. Finally, the rarest items and weapons are known as "legendary," and they are gold.

🔺 The number of stars associated with each level of rarity is also represented by a name and a color, with the most common being gray and the rarest being gold.

Short-Range Weapons

Short-range weapons are those you would use in close combat, when another player is only a few feet away. Short-range weapons are ineffective when used at medium or long range, meaning more than 10 feet or so away. The best place to use short-range weapons is inside buildings.

Pistol

⬆ Because the common pistol is the weakest weapon in the game, use it only if it's the only thing you have left.

The weakest short-range weapon in Fortnite is the pistol. Its low damage output means that it typically takes five or six shots to deal 100 damage to an opponent. The pistol is available only in the three lowest rarity tiers, common (gray), uncommon (green), and rare (blue).

Suppressed Pistol

⬆ When you fire the suppressed pistol, the shots are more difficult for other players to hear compared to a non-suppressed weapon.

New players of Fortnite often don't understand the difference between the suppressed and the normal pistol variations. Honestly, the difference is very small. Although the suppressed pistol is rarer than the generic one, being available in the highest two rarity tiers of epic (purple) and legendary (gold), that does not mean it is a strategic choice for battle. When you use the suppressed pistol, the only people you will have a slight advantage over are the people using the regular pistol.

Revolver

◆ You will see the revolver in common (gray), uncommon (green), and rare (blue) varieties.

The revolver is similar to the pistol in the amount of damage it does, but it has an added bonus of being able to kill opponents without shields with one shot to the head. However, because of this advantage, the revolver only holds six medium bullets at a time, has a larger amount of recoil, and fires far slower.

Hand Cannon

⬆ The biggest difference between the revolver and the hand cannon is that the hand cannon can potentially eliminate players with one head shot, no matter how much health and shield they have. In order for you to kill someone with one head shot with the revolver, your opponent can't have any shield.

The hand cannon is a pistol that fires heavy bullets at your opponents and does large amounts of damage. The main difference between the hand cannon and the revolver is that the hand cannon fires heavy bullets instead of medium bullets (which the revolver uses), kills enemies with 100 health *and* 100 shield in two or three shots, and is available in the top two tiers of rarity: epic (purple) and legendary (gold).

Tactical Shotgun

⬆ At the start of the game, make sure you always have a shotgun by picking one up as soon as you see it.

Overall, shotguns are one of the most useful weapons to have in Fortnite. The tactical shotgun is the weakest shotgun, but it fires faster than the rest of the shotguns. Since this weapon is available only in the bottom three rarity tiers, you have to make sure to shoot often and aim for the head when using this weapon.

Pump Shotgun

⬢ **Having a shotgun at the start of the game is extremely useful because very few players will have shields (see Chapter 6).**

The pump shotgun is similar to the tactical shotgun except that it fires slower but more powerful shots. One downside is that it needs to be reloaded after five shots. While using the pump shotgun, make sure you move around—meaning jumping, not just running—so that your enemy has trouble aiming at you while you're so close to each other. The pump shotgun is available in the uncommon (green) and rare (blue) rarities.

Heavy Shotgun

⏷ The heavy shotgun is like the tactical shotgun and pump shotgun combined. It holds seven shots, fires quickly, and has better range than any of the other shotguns.

The heavy shotgun is the most powerful shotgun in the game. When using the gun, which comes in epic (purple) and legendary (gold) rarities, players can kill an opponent in two shots from a farther distance, and faster, than with the pump shotgun. With this gun in your inventory, you are sure to win most shotgun battles.

Suppressed Submachine Gun

⏷ The suppressed submachine gun fires very quickly but gets more inaccurate the longer you fire it.

The suppressed submachine gun uses light ammunition to quickly fire several low-damage rounds at close-range opponents. When using this gun, make sure you're aiming down your sights by holding the right-click button on the PC or the left trigger on the Xbox or PlayStation console in order to compensate for the gun's large recoil with each bullet.

Tactical Submachine Gun

Epic | Ranged Weapon
TACTICAL SUBMACHINE GUN
Ranged
Ammo: Light Bullets
35   ★★★★

E
Swap
equipped

The tactical submachine gun does more damage and has less recoil than the suppressed submachine gun, which makes it more powerful.

Better than the suppressed submachine gun, the tactical submachine gun deals a slight bit of extra damage with less recoil. When using the gun, which comes in uncommon (green), rare (blue), and epic (purple) rarities, be sure to capitalize on this weapon's clean-up effectivity. In other words, use this weapon to rush critically wounded opponents.

Medium-Range Weapons

Anytime you're outside a building is the right time to consider using a medium-range weapon. If you use a medium-range weapon at short range, your shooting will be much less accurate. Using it at longer ranges will also be less accurate. Assault rifles that are not burst rifles are preferred because they are easier to tap-fire with, which is more accurate (see Chapter 8).

Burst Assault Rifle

Common | Ranged Weapon
BURST ASSAULT RIFLE
🏹 Ranged | Assault
📶 Ammo: Medium Bullets
30 ★ LV 10
E Pick up

🔼 **The burst assault rifle fires three bullets every one time you shoot. Only the first bullet will be 100 percent accurate, whereas the other two will be random.**

The burst assault rifle uses medium ammunition to quickly fire a burst of three rounds at medium- to long-range opponents. When using the gun, which comes in common (gray), uncommon (green), and rare (blue) rarities, be mindful there is a notable recoil and a wide spread unless you are aiming down your sight.

Assault Rifle (M16)

⬆ Unless you come across a SCAR—a more rare assault rifle that acts just like a semiautomatic—this is the best assault rifle to use in most situations. Many players refer to this weapon as the M16 because it is designed to look like an M16 assault rifle.

The semiautomatic assault rifle uses medium ammunition to fire rounds at medium- to long-range opponents. When using the gun, which comes in common (gray), uncommon (green), and rare (blue) rarities, fire with slow, steady consistency while aiming down your sight for maximum effectiveness.

Assault Rifle (SCAR)

⬆ This is the best assault rifle in the game because it does the most damage and has the least amount of recoil of all the assault rifles. Most players refer to this gun as the SCAR because its design is based on the real-life FN-SCAR assault rifle.

The SCAR uses medium ammunition to fire rounds exceptionally accurately at medium- to long-range opponents. When using the gun, which comes in epic (purple) and legendary (gold) rarities, be sure to take advantage of its notable accuracy at range.

Hunting Rifle

⬥ **The hunting rifle acts similar to a sniper rifle without the scope. Because it does not have a scope, it is useful when you're not sure if your target is at medium or long range.**

The hunting rifle, which comes in uncommon (green) and rare (blue) rarities, uses heavy ammunition to fire powerful rounds at medium- to long-range opponents. This weapon works on a bolt-action system, meaning once you fire one bullet you have to reload, so be sure to choose your shots wisely.

Minigun

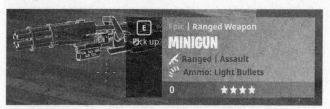

⬥ **Refrain from using this weapon directly on enemies. Instead, use it to shoot out the bottoms of enemy bases. It fires very quickly and you never have to reload as long as you have ammo, but that also means it is very inaccurate.**

The minigun uses small ammunition to fire unlimited rounds (until you run out) with no cooldown times. When using the gun, which comes in epic (purple) and legendary (gold) rarities, don't stand out in the open for too long or you will get shot. If you have the ammunition to support it, this weapon can be useful for destroying opposing bases for as long as you hold the trigger while your opponents panic to rebuild.

Light Machine Gun

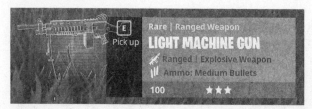

Rare | Ranged Weapon
LIGHT MACHINE GUN
Ranged | Explosive Weapon
Ammo: Medium Bullets
100 ★★★

Pick up E

▲ **The light machine gun comes in two rarities, rare (blue) and epic (purple). When using this gun, make sure that you are compensating for its high amount of recoil by slowly aiming down more and more the longer you fire it.**

The light machine gun works similar to the minigun with its high fire rate and high damage to enemy structures. However, the light machine gun uses medium bullets instead of small bullets (like the minigun) and has a magazine size of 100 bullets. Once your magazine runs out, you will have to spend a far longer time reloading than with other weapons.

Long-Range Weapons

If you aim down your sight with a medium-range weapon and your enemy is too small to see clearly, you should use a long-range weapon instead. Near the end of the game, when you are likely to be in your base and opponents are likely to be in theirs, there is a good chance someone else is aiming at you with a long-range weapon. So make sure you duck before and right after you take every shot.

Assault Rifle with Scope

Rare | Ranged Weapon
ASSAULT RIFLE WITH SCOPE
Ranged | Assault
Ammo: Medium Bullets
20 ★★★

▲ **This weapon fires the fastest of the long-range weapons but does the least damage.**

The scoped assault rifle uses medium ammunition and utilizes a magnified optic to fire at opponents at medium to long range with ease. When using the gun, which comes in rare (blue) and epic (purple) rarities, be aware that this is not a weapon you should use at short range when you're on the defensive. Always take the time at close range to switch weapons.

Semiautomatic Sniper Rifle

Legendary | Ranged Weapon
SEMI-AUTO SNIPER RIFLE
Ranged | Sniper Rifle
Ammo: Heavy Bullets
E Pick up
9 ★★★★★ LV 20

◆ The semiautomatic sniper rifle usually takes two or three shots to kill, making it less effective than the bolt-action sniper rifle.

Although weaker than its bolt-action counterpart, the semi-automatic sniper rifle uses a magnified optic and heavy ammunition to critically damage your opponents at medium to long range. When using the weapon, which comes in epic (purple) and legendary (gold), be sure to take advantage of the firing speed this particular rifle offers.

Bolt-Action Sniper Rifle

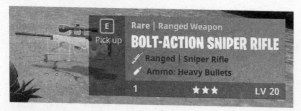

Rare | Ranged Weapon
BOLT-ACTION SNIPER RIFLE
Ranged | Sniper Rifle
Ammo: Heavy Bullets
E Pick up
1 ★★★ LV 20

◆ You have to reload after every shot with the bolt-action sniper rifle, which is a disadvantage, but there is a high likelihood that your shot will kill your enemy with one hit.

The bolt-action sniper rifle uses a magnified optic and heavy ammunition to fire at opponents at medium to long range with ease. The gun, which comes in rare (blue), epic (purple), and legendary (gold) rarities, is not a good choice at short range because of the slow bolt-action reset time.

Launchers

Launchers are the best choice as a weapon at medium range when you are attempting to destroy enemy bases and all the players in them. Typically, launchers are hard to find but are very useful.

Grenade Launcher

⌃ The grenade launcher is the best choice when the enemy base is large. Since it lobs several grenades, it is useful for destroying lots of structures quickly.

The grenade launcher lobs rockets toward opponents at close to medium range. When using this weapon, which comes in rare (blue), epic (purple), and legendary (gold) rarities, take advantage of the ability to ricochet the grenades off any surface, as the grenades detonate not upon impact but at a fixed time from their launch.

Rocket Launcher

▲ The rocket launcher fires one rocket at a time and is very accurate.

The rocket launcher fires rockets at opponents at short, medium, and even long range. When using this weapon, which comes in rare (blue), epic (purple), and legendary (gold) rarities, understand that the rockets fire at a slower speed than you might expect. Essentially, it is a slow but accurate weapon.

As you can tell, all weapons in Fortnite can be useful, but choose wisely based on distance and situation. Not every weapon is perfect for every situation.

Epic Games is constantly adding more weapons to Fortnite, which you'll hear about as soon as you log into the game. Make sure you're the first to know if anything new is released by Epic so that you can take the time to study the new weaponry and learn how to use it most effectively. Most gunfights in Fortnite are won by the player who comes into the fight with a weapon more adequately suited for the circumstance.

CHAPTER 6

Healing, Grenades, and Utilities

Healing supplies, throwables, and utilities are a huge part of Fortnite Battle Royale. Healing supplies allow you to recover after you have been wounded, grenades are a powerful weapon for attacking your opponents, and with the variety of utilities in Fortnite, you can both inflict damage on your opponents and heal yourself when you've been injured. All these tools are crucial to the game; you need to take advantage of them in order to dominate other contenders in the world of Fortnite.

Healing

There are two main types of healing devices—things you apply and things you drink. Each type of healing tool improves your health and/or your shield by a certain percentage, which varies by item. The better items take longer to consume.

Bandage

Bandages give you 15 percent health and take only four seconds to consume, which is another way to say "use." However, you can use bandages only if you are below 75 percent health because they only increase your total health to 75 percent. For example, if you are at 60 percent health, bandages will boost your health to 75 percent. If you are at 50 percent, they will boost it to 65 percent. But if you are at 80 percent—or any number above 75 percent—you will not be permitted to use a bandage.

⬆ There are five inventory slots total, and you can only hold up to 15 bandages in one slot of your inventory at a time.

Med Kit

No matter what health level you are, med kits will get you to 100 percent health. They take 10 seconds to consume.

⬆ You can only hold up to three med kits in one slot of your inventory at a time. You wouldn't want to fill all your inventory slots with too much of one healing device.

Shield Potion

Shield potions give you 50 percent shield and take five seconds to consume.

⬆ You can only hold one or two shield potions in one slot of your inventory at a time.

Small Shield Potion

Small shield potions give you 25 percent shield and take only two seconds to consume. However, you can't use these mini shields to get more than a total of 50 percent shield.

⬆ You can only hold up to 10 small shield potions in one slot of your inventory at a time.

Slurp Juice

Slurp juices will grant you a total of 25 percent shield and 25 percent health. After consuming a slurp juice, which takes two seconds, both your health and your shield will improve at a rate of about 1 percent per second.

⏶ You can only hold one or two slurp juices in one slot of your inventory at a time. These are helpful to use if you're in a hurry, since you have to stand still when you're consuming any potions, and slurp juice and the small shield potion take the least amount of time to activate.

Chug Jug

Chug jugs are the crown jewel of healing. Consuming one takes 15 seconds; however, no matter what level health you start with, at the end of those 15 seconds you will have 100 percent health and 100 percent shield.

⏶ You can only hold one chug jug in one slot of your inventory at a time.

Throwables

In contrast to healing tools, throwables are all weapons. Grenades do damage to both players and structures. Boogie bombs and impulse grenades don't inflict damage directly, but impulse grenades can cause damage if used at great height.

Grenade

Grenades are helpful tools on the battlefield. You can hold on to your shooting button to display an arc on your heads-up display (HUD) that the grenade will follow after you throw it.

⬆ The arc is useful for knowing where the item will go when it is thrown.

While you're holding the grenade, it will not go off. After you throw the grenade, it will detonate in three seconds. When it detonates, opponents in the immediate area will wish they weren't.

⏏ You can only hold up to 10 grenades in one slot of your inventory at a time.

Boogie Bomb

Boogie bombs are unique to Fortnite. You can hold on to your shooting button to display on your screen an arc that the boogie bomb will follow after you throw it. After you throw a boogie bomb, it will detonate the instant it makes contact with anything. When it detonates, any opponents in the immediate area will break out into dance for five seconds or until they take damage from being hit by a bullet, whichever comes first. This is a bomb, but it does not do any damage. When your opponents are essentially stunned for five seconds, they become a defenseless target, making them easy to eliminate.

⏏ You can only hold up to 10 boogie bombs in one slot of your inventory.

Impulse Grenade

While impulse grenades will not cause direct damage, they will launch you or other players in the opposite direction from where they detonate. You can use impulse grenades to get opponents out in the open or to escape from danger yourself; however, opponents will also use them on you.

To use an impulse grenade, hold on to your shooting button to display on your screen an arc that the impulse grenade will follow after you throw it. After you throw the impulse grenade, it will make contact with any object in the game, stick to it, and detonate after one second. When it detonates, any opponents within the immediate area will be launched into the air based upon their location relative to the impulse grenade. For example, if they are above the grenade, it will launch them up; if they are to the side of the grenade, it will launch them farther to the same side. The impulse grenades can also be used on yourself as a means of transport. You can do this by sprinting forward, aiming directly at the ground in front of you, throwing the impulse grenade, and then jumping shortly after. This will send you flying forward and help you to escape the incoming storm or enemy players. However, don't ignore the impulse grenade's effectiveness as a weapon. You can launch opponents off high points on the map and potentially kill them with the fall damage.

You can only hold up to 10 impulse grenades in one slot of your inventory.

Remote Explosives

Remote explosives are simply explosives you can place anywhere at any time and detonate remotely. They stick to any object in the game and can be set off by other explosives and bullets hitting them. You can hold on to your shooting button to display on your screen an arc that the remote explosive will follow after you throw it. Since the remote explosive has no set timer, you can just sit and wait until you see it detonate.

△ You can hold up to 10 remote explosives in one slot of your inventory.

Port-A-Fort

A port-a-fort is a grenade that you throw at the ground and it spawns a fort for you to occupy in battle. You can hold on to your shooting button to display on your screen an arc that the port-a-fort will follow after you throw it. A pre-made fort is instantly constructed at the impact point. If you are lucky enough to stumble upon a port-a-fort in a situation where you need cover immediately, you can quickly throw it at the ground instead of taking the time to build a fort piece by piece. Fully constructed, the port-a-fort is three stories tall and made entirely of metal. The bottom floor is one-by-one with a door for entry. Tires inside the bottom level allow you to jump on them to quickly get to the roof of the fort where you rain hell down on your opponents.

△ You can hold up to five port-a-forts in one slot of your inventory, but it's unlikely you would ever have more than one at a time.

Utilities

Utilities are a mix of weapons you can use to inflict damage on others, to hide yourself, or to move out of a situation quickly, either to get away from danger or to attack someone else.

Damage Trap

Damage traps can be laid down on any floor, wall, or ceiling in wait for an opponent to walk by. When an opponent walks on the block where the trap is set, it will deploy spikes that will critically damage and, in most cases, kill any opponent. Traps cannot be removed. The only way to purge the environment of a trap is to destroy the surface that the trap is occupying.

A trap can be used more than once, but you have to wait two seconds before triggering it a second time.

Launch Pad

Launch pads provide a way to travel a great distance in a short time. This is especially helpful if you need to get out of a bad situation quickly. Launch pads can only be placed on a floor you've built, not on an opponent's floor, so keep in mind that you'll need to first build your own floor before you can use a launch pad. To get the most out of a launch pad, set it down at a high elevation. This means building up and then setting down a floor to place it on. If the floor that the launch pad is on is destroyed, the launch pad will disappear.

⌃ The higher the launch pad is, the higher you will be launched and the farther you will be able to travel.

Cozy Campfire

Although cozy campfires can be laid only on a floor you've built, and not on one that has been created by an opponent, you and your squadmates standing near it can slowly regenerate health. This is another method to break past the 75 percent health limit that bandages enforce. It may be slow, but that extra health obtained from using a cozy campfire could mean the difference between life and death.

⌃ While cozy campfires are regenerative, like healing devices, they are stored in the trap inventory slot. Unlike other healing tools, however, they can heal several players at once.

Bush

⌃ There is no other tool in the game that can be used as a disguise.

The bush can be used as a disguise if you need to hide from opponents or if you are trying to sneak up on them. Although the disguise does take up a notable amount of space on your screen, because your character becomes much larger than before, the bush is effective for hiding in open fields. Once you take the form of a bush, you will stay that way until you take damage from an enemy.

Hop Rocks

⬣ Hop rocks can be found only in meteor impact craters throughout the map. The best place to go to find the most hop rocks is in Dusty Divot.

In season 4 of Fortnite Battle Royale, a meteor has struck the island in the location where Dusty Depot once stood strong. Now named Dusty Divot, the crater where the meteor hit the island holds a new crystal that can be consumed by players. Hop rocks holds a new consumable crystal that allows you to jump high in the air and experience a low-gravity effect for about 20 seconds before wearing off.

You can consume as many hop rocks as you can find in order to extend the time period of the helpful effect they have on your movement. When using a hop rock, you will glow a purple color and will hear a sonic-boom-like sound every time you (or any nearby players) jump into the air.

⬆ What a player looks like when jumping through the sky while using a hop rock. Although hop rocks give a movement advantage to players that use them, the players also have the disadvantage of being heard when jumping and glowing a purple color. It is easy to tell if a player is using a hop rock or not.

With all these tools at your disposal, on top of the arsenal of weapons you can acquire and structures you can build for protection and attacks, your chances of emerging victorious increase. The main thing to focus on, however, is not acquiring all these resources, but using them to your advantage. There's no method to finding particular weapons or tools—it's all random. So pick up what you can when you see it, but don't spend too much time hunting for specific items.

CHAPTER 7

Landing

Every game of Fortnite starts with you boarding a flying blue school bus, also known as a Battle Bus. While on the bus, you will want to look at the map of the island and decide where, ideally, you want to land. This choice will determine whether you get good loot and increase your odds of surviving versus being one of the first players eliminated right out of the gate. If you don't use the map to chart your course, you will be effectively pushed out of the bus when the timer on the bus hits zero and the game will start whether you're ready or not. It's smarter to take your fate into your own hands rather than just let the game determine when you jump.

After choosing where to land, players jump out of the bus and start to skydive down to the island beneath them. Here are the techniques, tips, and tricks to landing successfully.

Choosing Where to Land

Where you decide to land is entirely your choice. However, there are good destinations and not-so-good destinations. The path of the Battle Bus, which is shown to you in the

pregame lobby before the game starts, is a key
factor in determining how many players go to
certain locations on the map. For the most
part, if the path of the Battle Bus flies
directly over a named location, there is a
high probability that several players will choose
to land there, because they can get to the ground fast
and start looting.

Because of the opportunity for a speedy landing, the
majority of players opt to land at locations close to the
center of the map. Locations on the outside edges of the
island, like Junk Junction, Moisty Mire, and Flush Factory,
almost never have players landing near them. At the same
time, locations like Retail Row, Salty Springs, and *especially*
Tilted Towers, which are near the center of the island, always
have a bunch of players landing at them because the Battle
Bus is more likely to fly over them. Tilted Towers is by far the
location with the largest number of initial players—between
25 and 50 players always choose to land here in every game.
If you're someone who prefers a high-risk, high-reward
scenario, land at Tilted Towers; you will have the chance to
eliminate many opponents right away. However, if you aren't
very skilled yet and want to encounter only a few players in
each game while you learn how to utilize building and weaponry, landing toward the outside of the map is a good idea.

Dropping Out of the Battle Bus

Once your player is spawned on the pregame island outside
of the main map—the waiting area to board the Battle Bus—
you should open up your map by pressing Tab on your PC or
the Menu button on Xbox and pressing down on the gamepad
on PlayStation. The first thing you will see is the path of the

Battle Bus across the island, as well as an icon of the Battle Bus that represents its current location on the map.

Within the map you are able to place a marker on the location where you would like to land, and you can also see the other markers your teammates have placed. The white pointer on the map is your marker tool, and you can add a mark on the map by left-clicking on your PC or by pressing A on Xbox or Circle on PlayStation. To move the marker around, use your analog sticks if playing on a console or your mouse if playing on a PC. Markers are useful for communication and pointing out specific locations of other players in the game (if, for example, you are playing as a team and your teammate is having trouble locating the other players). Because the map is so large, you can zoom in and out by using the scroll wheel on your PC or the left and right triggers on your console.

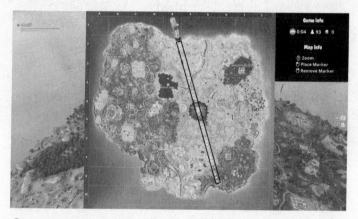

▲ The arrows show the path the Battle Bus will follow as it travels across the island. The path will always be straight and will almost always cross one of the four grid squares in the center of the map.

On the map you will notice a set of grid lines, labeled with letters and numbers on the top and left-hand side of the border. These grids are very useful for calling out locations to teammates when traveling between safe zones in-game. As a general rule, try not to pick landing locations that are more than three grid boxes away from the location where you plan to drop out of the Battle Bus. You don't necessarily exit the bus and immediately drop to your chosen destination; you have to glide a while in between as well. As you will soon learn in skydiving, it is very difficult to land quickly and gain that head start to looting if the location where you drop out of the bus is very far away.

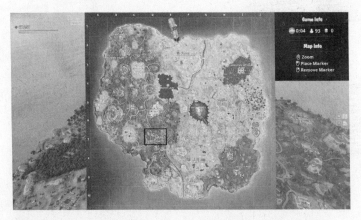

⬢ By marking a location on your map, Shifty Shafts in this example, you can find your designated drop location much faster and easier if you lose your orientation while skydiving.

Using your marking tool even when you're playing as a solo player can be helpful as well. When you place a marker on the map and then close the map, there will be a blue tick on the top center of your screen along your compass that shows you exactly which direction you should be facing in order to

reach your mark. If you want to place your marker somewhere else, just select another location. Unfortunately, you
cannot place more than one marker at a time.

How to Skydive Effectively

In Fortnite, the main way to get where you want to go at the
beginning of the game, when the Battle Bus is flying you overhead, is to wait for the bus to arrive as close to your desired
location as possible and simply jump. Sometimes, however,
that isn't enough. Being able to land in a populated area
before your opponents do is important.

**⏺ For beginning players, aiming to land at small locations,
like unnamed factories, may be the best option to ensure
survival during the first frenzied
moments as players hit the
ground and start trying
to eliminate other
players.**

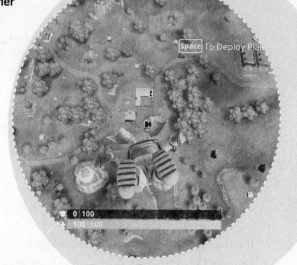

There are a few tricks you can use while you are landing to ensure you're landing as fast as possible. First of all, jump out of the bus early. Before you actually exit the bus, try to estimate how far you will be able to travel with your glider, which acts as a parachute, before you hit the ground. Then, when you are out of the bus, nose-dive by holding W on the PC or pushing the left stick forward on Xbox One or PlayStation while you are looking straight down. While you are nose-diving, aim for the lowest point in the map, such as between mountains and rivers. After your glider is forced out, aim to land on something high, but not too high, such as a rooftop, so you can jump off it and proceed to loot.

Now, let's say you want to travel to a location far away from the bus that you couldn't reach by skydiving; there is a trick. If you repeatedly hit the button that allows you to switch between your glider and skydiving as fast as you can—A on Xbox One, Circle on PlayStation 4, or the space bar on your PC—you will appear to barely descend while still maintaining the same speed you would have as if you were gliding forward. This method could take a while before you hit the ground, but you can travel the farthest distance by using it. Furthermore, using this method can potentially grant you access to parts of the map where nobody else will land. This introduces the possibility that you'll be able to loot stress-free for a few minutes with no one else nearby. Remember to stay aware of where other players are landing near you by looking up above you as you're gliding to earth; never be too comfortable.

Now, if you decide not to go far from the Battle Bus, but you can tell that just nose-diving and gliding will cause you to land a bit short of your desired location, hop out of the bus when you are closest to said location, and when diving through the sky, hold W on your PC or push the left stick forward on Xbox One and PlayStation, while you are looking down at about a 45-degree angle. This is the sweet spot in the world of landing as it does not take much away from the speed of your descent, but it adds a good amount of distance to your journey before you hit the ground.

Pay attention to your surroundings as you land. If you're new to Fortnite, your familiarity with your surroundings is the most important part of landing, as it will help you find loot quickly and get the jump on people once you acquire that loot. If you want to learn more about an area, you should land there in order to learn how to play the area to your advantage.

First Instincts Once on the Ground

When you first land, you are going to want to find your way to loot as quickly as possible. Landing on a rooftop and breaking your way down through the roof with your pickaxe will be the most effective way of acquiring loot before nearby opponents who may choose to land on the ground level and walk through the front door. Walking through a door is much easier and quicker than chopping through a roof with an axe. Not only will you have the high ground, as you are above them, but, in most instances, you will also have gotten your hands on some form of weaponry before them, since there are many chests just under the rooftops, often in attics. Be sure to study the map and learn where chests spawn as you play the game more and more.

As you land and begin acquiring loot, you may find the occasional trap lying on the ground. Do not hesitate to use it—it may save your life and help you acquire more loot. If you land and the first thing you find is a trap while enemies are on their way to your house with weapons, set down that trap between you and them and hope they set it off. If all goes well, you will have your first kill of the game, plus all of that person's loot. Do not take your traps for granted as they are immensely useful tools in this game.

Be sure to observe your surroundings during landing and come up with a decent estimate not only of how many people are landing with you at any particular named location, but also of where, specifically, they are landing. This will help you decide where to push ahead and when to try to avoid challenging the opposing forces around you.

Never land and try to race people to loot who are lower than you—meaning already on the ground. You should never intentionally allow yourself to be in a position of disadvantage. No matter how confident you are, disadvantages will eventually lead to failure. If you realize that the location where you had planned to land is being taken over by opponents already on the ground, try your best to quickly adjust your landing to find a safer place to begin your game.

When you are landing in a close-quarters environment like a house or another building, try your hardest to find a shotgun. Shotguns in close situations, especially at the start of the game, are a must. If you are facing an early engagement where one person has a shotgun and the other doesn't, you had better pray you are the one with the shotgun. Relying on a shotgun early in the game can also bring the opportunity to play stealthily—the chance to wait for people to enter your house or building unknowingly, giving you the advantage of surprise.

When beginning looting, the main thing you are going to want to take into account, other than your weapons, is your resources. As you rummage through your landing zone, don't ignore the furniture, rocks, and trees as these are all useful sources of materials. All these things, when struck by your pickaxe, give you useful resources in early engagements.

You can gain an advantage in early situations when you have materials to build and your opponents do not. In most instances, fights like these will always end in the death of the least experienced player. Never forget that building is your biggest tool in the game. Always try to avoid fighting without resources so that you have the option to build your way out of a sticky situation.

CHAPTER 8

Combat

I n every game of Fortnite, you'll come in contact with other players who are trying to win the game just like you. However, since only one player can claim Victory Royale, all others must be eliminated. How you knock out your opponents is entirely your choice, but the most effective way to eliminate them is by using the weapons you've gathered while looting.

To help you become more efficient and effective at eliminating your competitors as soon as you see them in the game, here are some tips for pursuing fellow players and also avoiding elimination yourself.

Firing Your Weapon

No matter what weapon you use to fire at your opponent, there will be an effect on the direction of the bullets called "bloom."

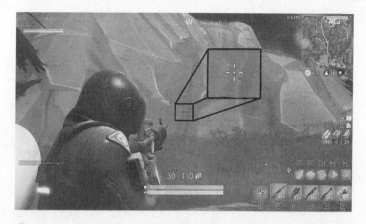

⬆ This is a picture of your reticle, which is what you look through during the game to plan where to fire your gun.

⬆ This is a picture of the bloom effect. Notice how the bullet—the white star-shaped image inside the larger box—does not land in the center of the reticle but rather down and to the right of the center.

This feature was added into the game in order to make combat more balanced by making the accuracy of the bullets slightly random. So when you fire a single shot from your weapon (whatever kind of gun you're using), the bullet will not go completely straight. The bullets will always stay within the frame of the crosshair—the faint circle with four dots in it—in the center of the screen, but they will not always land on the center dot in the very center of the crosshair, even if you're an extremely accurate shot. This randomness makes the game more exciting and prevents experienced players from completely dominating from the outset, which would make the action less enjoyable for everyone else.

The crosshair at the center of your screen will get wider and then shrink every time you fire a bullet. If you fire your weapon too fast, by clicking your Fire button (right trigger on Xbox and PlayStation and left click on the PC), the crosshair will expand, causing your bullets to fly even less accurately. This feature is called "recoil" or "mechanic."

Every time you engage in combat with another player and fire your weapon, it is important to remember that your aim, bloom, and recoil are the largest factors in determining who is victorious. Assuming neither you nor your enemy builds a form of cover, which we'll talk about shortly, and instead both of you focus on firing at each other out in the open, the player who can aim and control recoil better will win 67 percent of the time. Of course, there is always a 33 percent chance that other opponents get lucky and have less bloom than you, causing their bullets to go straighter.

The first thing you can do to improve your odds of winning a gunfight with another player is to practice controlling your recoil. Most often you will be using a semiautomatic assault rifle to fire at your opponents, unless they are very close or very far away from you. The semiautomatic assault rifle is considered the best weapon to use in combat, so it's the one you should learn how to handle first.

When practicing, you should try to fire as accurately as possible by using a technique known as "tapping." You can tap while aiming down the sights of your weapon by pressing the left trigger on your controller if you're playing on a console or by holding the right mouse button if playing on a PC and firing only when your crosshair recoil is done resetting. It may take a couple of rounds to recognize how quickly the crosshair resets. In order to master tapping, focus on remembering the rhythm of the crosshair resetting so you can fire quickly with more precision. While tapping, it is also helpful to crouch and move your player left and right every couple of shots. Players who can master the skill of tapping are able to win many more gunfights thanks to better accuracy.

How to Use Building to Win Every Battle

One of Fortnite's unique features is the building mechanic—that is, the ability to build structures on the fly for protection and visibility. Players are able to construct and edit their own walls, ramps, floors (or ceilings), and pyramids. This means that players always have a way to create their own cover when being attacked or to gain a height advantage when attacking other players.

Assuming you're the attacking player, the first thing you should always do to maximize the chances of winning a battle is to build ramps (assuming you have resources available), which will allow you to gain a height advantage (see Chapter 4). Your opponent may then build ramps as well. In that case, instead of just building one or two of your own, either keep building up or shoot at the bottom ramp of the person attacking you. Shooting at the base of any structure will cause the entire structure to collapse.

Once you have the advantage, peek over the top of your cover and tap-fire your assault rifle until any opponents nearby are eliminated.

⬆ **The screenshot shows a close-up of the health and shield bar. The health bar is the gauge on the bottom and the shield bar is the gauge on the top.**

Once the battle is over, take a moment to build a square fort around yourself with walls and use whatever bandages, medical kits, or shield potions you were carrying to regain any health you may have lost. You can monitor your health by looking at the green gauge at the bottom of your screen. If you weren't carrying any bandages, check the loot of your fallen enemies to see if they had any you can use; it's not like they are going to need it!

Using the Safe Zone to Your Advantage

As every game of Fortnite begins to wind down, with fewer and fewer players left, the play area becomes noticeably more compact, making it harder for a large number of players to stay alive. Also, most of the players who are still alive near the end will probably have very powerful weapons, such as rocket launchers. They will frequently use these powerful weapons to shoot at the bases of the structures other players have built and thus expose their opponents.

The best way to ensure your survival late in the game is to make sure you are in the safe zone and have a base built as soon as possible. If you are not in the next safe zone and need to get there, don't just run straight and out in the open; instead, use your time to cautiously rotate along the outer edge of the play area until you are confident that you are safe.

⏏ As the safe zone—the dark outer circle in this photo— shrinks, you want to be as close as possible to the white circle on the inside so that you have as much time as possible to get into the safe zone. The outer circle shrinks at different rates— faster where it is farther from the white circle and slower where it is close. So you don't want to be by the X, where the safe zone is shrinking faster, but by the check mark, where it is shrinking slower.

Attacking Other Players' Bases and Defending Your Own

Like you, other opponents will have their own towering bases in the later stages of the game so that they can protect themselves and see large portions of the play area from above. This strategy works. However, that means it is harder for other players, like you, to win.

In order to counter this tactic, frequently used by skilled players, the trick is to focus on shooting out the foundation of their fortress, rather than getting into sniping wars with them as they quickly poke their head out of the top of their base.

The best way to destroy any structure is by using explosives. Weapons such as rocket launchers and grenade launchers will yield the best results, meaning the tower falling in the shortest amount of time. Unfortunately, these weapons are not very common. However, there are other explosives like the throwable grenade that also work well. The downside of using handheld explosives is that you have to be much closer to the enemy's base to use them effectively. Lastly, if you or your teammates don't have any explosives, the last resort option is to simply shoot out the structure with your assault rifles.

Once you find and destroy the bottom of these often massive forts, the rest of the fort will crumble. This is extremely effective against players who build their bases too high into the clouds. One rule of thumb is to avoid building bases more than three or four stories above the ground. Building too high is dangerous because when bases are destroyed the players sitting at the top will have their floor fall out from underneath them, and they will usually take a large amount of fall damage—meaning they will come close to death due to their injuries.

In order to avoid dying from fall damage, use this chart to tell how much damage you will receive when falling from different building heights. The closer you get to 100 percent damage, the closer you are to death and elimination from the game, so you want to keep your damage as low as possible—preferably none. Building more than six levels above the ground will put you at extreme risk of dying from fall damage if your base is destroyed. Falling damage affects only your green health bar, not your shields. Here is the damage you will sustain when you fall from structures of different heights; the more levels your structure has, the more damage you sustain when you fall:

HEIGHT	DAMAGE
1	None
2	None
3	None
4	15–20%
5	45–50%
6	95–100%
7	>100% (death)

If you are outside of the next safe zone and need to get into it, or maybe you even see another base you could take over, a great tool you can use is the launch pad. This purple trampoline-like object can be used an unlimited number of times once placed on a floor. You should know that in order to get the maximum usage out of it, it's smart to place it at high elevations; sometimes you may even have to build up

five or six stories. Place the launch pad down by pressing
F5 on your keyboard if playing on a PC, X then B on Xbox, or
Triangle then Circle on PlayStation.

⏶ This screenshot shows a player skydiving toward another
player's base after using a launch pad.

Once you've used your launch pad and you are flying with
your glider, just aim to land behind the players you plan on
attacking. Once you've landed, then use your shotgun to
dominate your opponents in a close-range confrontation.
They won't know what hit them.

TIPS AND TRICKS

CHAPTER 9

Battle Pass

What is the Battle Pass? It is a tool that allows you to acquire exclusive, limited-time cosmetic items during a single season in Fortnite Battle Royale. The cost? Battle Passes cost 950 V-Bucks, or $9.50, and can only be purchased (you can't earn them or win them). Be sure to get your hands on the Battle Pass if you are fond of a particular cosmetic item, because after that season, it will never be available again. Not within the item shop, not as a special promotion— it will simply disappear.

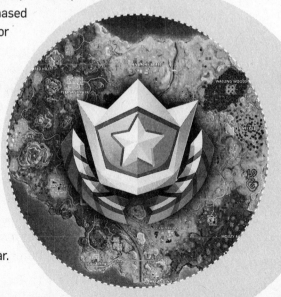

The Battle Pass is a way to keep the game fresh by introducing a range of limited-edition cosmetic items. In addition, the Battle Pass provides a percentage multiplier that can help you get to the next level in the game more quickly. That is, each Battle Pass comes with incentives at each level in the game. When you move up a tier, based on playing time and completing weekly challenges, a Battle Pass can provide freebies that make the game more interesting. Additionally, the Battle Pass can provide a percentage multiplier of your experience points, which is what it takes to move up a level, making it faster and easier to level up than without a Battle Pass.

Every 10 weeks there is a new "season" of Fortnite when the rewards available through a Battle Pass change. As of April 30, 2018, Fortnite will be starting its fourth Battle Pass season. Every time a season ends, players must buy a new Battle Pass in order to be able to play for the rewards of the next season.

There is a difference between the level you play at in the game and the tier you have earned in the Battle Pass. Moving up tiers, based on play and completing weekly challenges, earns you freebies in the Battle Pass. It has no impact on your level within the game itself, however.

Stars are the way in which you progress through the tiers of your Battle Pass. You start at tier 1 and can move up to tier 100, as of season 3. It takes 10 stars to progress to the next tier of your Battle Pass. By completing weekly and daily challenges, which earn you experience points and stars, and by gaining more playing experience, which rewards you with stars, you have the opportunity to max out your Battle Pass, reach tier 100, and earn all that there is to earn that season.

Through the Battle Pass, you are also able to earn V-Bucks to spend. However, when you get your hands on V-Bucks, you may not want to spend them right away. Though the basic Battle Pass costs 950 V-Bucks, you can opt for an upgraded version that costs 2,800 V-Bucks and automatically gives you all the rewards up to tier 25, so that instead of starting at tier 1, you start at tier 25.

Why is this important in regard to spending V-Bucks? If you want to spend as little money as possible, you could buy one Battle Pass and, instead of spending any V-Bucks you earn, you could then use those V-Bucks to buy the following season's Battle Pass. You can then continue that cycle each subsequent season. For example, for completing season 3 you earn 1,300 V-Bucks, which is more than enough to buy the Battle Pass for season 4, which costs 950 V-Bucks.

If saving money isn't a good enough reason for you to save the V-Bucks you earn, you can save them to use when an amazing cosmetic item drops into the item shop. Each tier of your Battle Pass costs 150 V-Bucks. This means that as you progress through your Battle Pass, you can propel your-self even further with the V-Bucks you earn. You never know when those spare V-Bucks may come in handy. Be sure to think long and hard before you spend your V-Bucks.

What Are the Pros of the Battle Pass?

You may be wondering whether a Battle Pass is worth getting your hands on. The answer is yes, definitely. No question.

The reason? For one, you will have more to do in the game. With all the potential rewards that can be unlocked and weekly challenges that the Battle Pass provides, you will be spending more time on the game just to complete these challenges and earn the rewards. Also, as you get farther and farther through your Battle Pass, you are rewarded with experience point boosts.

The Battle Pass also brings in a new ranking system. Similar to reaching a higher level in the game by earning experience points, you can also—but only with the Battle Pass—earn your way to new tiers by earning stars. Stars are available only when you level up by completing challenges in Fortnite. Earning your way through tiers, while it may be tedious, can be super satisfying when you make it to where you want to be.

Since the Battle Pass introduces new cosmetic items each season, it is a plus to be granted exclusive gear for spending time on the game. With the prices of cosmetic items valued at up to 2,000 V-Bucks, the cheapest Battle Pass, at 950 V-Bucks, is a steal considering the number of items you can unlock if you put the time into the game to earn them.

What Are the Cons of the Battle Pass?

Just because the Battle Pass offers so much, however, doesn't necessarily mean it is all great. Whether purchasing a Battle Pass and all of its goodies makes sense for you comes down to your personal preference. You may not be fond of any of the items within the tier unlocks of the Battle Pass. This means you may not see the value in the purchase as the challenges and experience point boosts may not be worth much to you.

Remember, Fortnite is free to play, which is a huge reason the game blew up to become what it is. No matter what platform you are occupying, you can get your hands on Fortnite and get right into the action at no cost. To put it simply, if the main reason you got Fortnite was because it was free, the thought of putting money into the game may not be appealing.

Let's face it—some of us do not have a lot of free time or money on our hands. This means that after purchasing a Battle Pass, you may not be able to get your money's worth if you won't be able to put the time in to earn your way through the tiers. However, even if you don't have a lot of time to put in, you can still get to the end of your Battle Pass and claim all the loot, for a price. One hundred and fifty V-Bucks per tier may not sound like much, but 100 tiers later, depending on your personal circumstances, your bank account may not be fond of you. If you are going to commit to the Battle Pass on Fortnite, be sure that you will have the time or money to get the most out of it; otherwise, you may not want to get the Battle Pass at all.

Leveling Up

If you choose not to purchase the Battle Pass, don't worry—the Battle Pass isn't Epic Games' only way to give you tasks to complete. You will still be able to level up in the game during the season. This feature comes with its own rewards as well. Each season what you can earn will differ. However, you can be certain it will be nowhere near your potential earnings as a Battle Pass holder. If you were looking forward to a ton of new challenges during the season, you won't get anywhere near as many challenges as you would with the Battle Pass. Each level is harder and harder to get through because each one requires more and more experience points.

Once you level up, the tracing that borders your custom banner will change in appearance to convey your ranking that season. At the beginning of every season, similar to tiers for Battle Pass holders, your rank will reset to level 1. Each season is a new ball game. If spending the money on the Battle Pass isn't something you want to do, just know you still have this alternative to fulfill any desire you may want to accomplish.

◆ You can see the rewards of both the free pass, which every player has, and the Battle Pass under the Battle Pass tab on the main menu. This page allows you to scroll through all the rewards you will be able to receive for leveling up your Battle Pass over time by doing things such as completing challenges.

All Things Considered, Is the Battle Pass Worth Getting?

With all the above points taken into consideration, if the Battle Pass is something you can afford, it is certainly worth getting. To start, the many hours of game time required to earn your way through the Battle Pass will keep you engaged, and the tremendous number of cosmetic items you can acquire, ranging from outfits to loading screens, will be worth $9.50. On top of that, the challenges you are tasked with to earn stars and experience points toward leveling up and arriving at new tiers, the experience point boosts that are granted only through the Battle Pass, and the V-Bucks you earn that total more than the base price of the Battle Pass all add up to way more than the purchase price.

Epic Games has been doing a stellar job in the cosmetic department, keeping people happy with all the new skins. If history repeats itself, the company will continue to outdo itself each season. Depending on your taste in skins, this means you will almost never be disappointed with what the Battle Pass provides the following season. If you bought and complete the base version, even if you are disappointed, you still earn more V-Bucks back than you spent on it. That is, you are spending 950 V-Bucks to get more than 950 V-Bucks back at the end, not to mention all the perks and bonuses that come with it. By this logic, Epic Games is paying you to get the Battle Pass and fully experience the game in the way the company hopes you will.

The best part is that all your earnings from the Battle Pass during a particular season are limited-time exclusives that will never make an appearance in the item shop. You thus get bragging rights over those who never got their hands on the Battle Pass during an earlier season to get a skin they wanted when you did. If you are looking for that exclusiveness in your Fortnite experience, as of season 3, nothing grants that level of exclusiveness more than the Battle Pass.

Ultimately, deciding whether you should get Fortnite's Battle Pass comes down to time more than the actual expense. If you have the time to sit down and power through the tiers of the Battle Pass, thus gaining the value of the money you spend on it, there is really no downside other than the money it initially costs. All in all, the Battle Pass is packed full of content each season that surpasses its face value, based on the prices of outfits and emotes in the item shop alone—even without including the V-Bucks that you make back. Of course, as you should with any purchase, make sure you want it before you buy it.

CHAPTER 10

Cosmetics

As you've been playing Fortnite, you may have noticed that many of the people you encounter are outfitted with unique items that differ greatly from the default appearances in the game. These items, called cosmetics, are variations you can acquire and incorporate into your game, from banners and outfits to back bling (items that go on players' backs), harvesting tools, skydiving trails, gliders, loading screens, and emotes. They can be obtained, sometimes for a price, from Twitch (a website used by popular gamers to broadcast themselves playing online games) events, new Battle Passes that are introduced every season in the game, the in-game store where items become available for purchase for a brief time, and even rare special events where skins are given out for free.

One example of a free skin available to the public is the Blue Team Leader outfit, which is still available now (at the time of this writing) in the PlayStation store on PS4. To get this fashionable outfit, if it's still available, go to the store and search for "Fortnite Battle Royale—: PlayStation Plus Celebration Pack."

⏶ This is what the Blue Team Leader outfit looks like. This outfit is unique simply because of the blue hat the player wears.

Cosmetic items are a way to taunt your victims, intimidate your opponents, and spice up the game to make it more entertaining. Most of the cosmetic items available in Fortnite are appealing, so don't hesitate to get new skins when they become available in-game. They may or may not return to the item shop, so if the one you like is there and you can afford it, get it while you can.

V-Bucks

The Battle Pass and cosmetic items in Fortnite are available only through special promotions or by paying with the in-game currency, V-Bucks. V-Bucks can only be obtained with real-world currency. This is how Epic Games, the maker of Fortnite, is able to profit from its free game. One hundred V-Bucks is worth $1.00, or $.01 per V-Buck.

⬆ One nice thing about the price of V-Bucks is that you get a slight discount if you buy them in bulk. Also it's important to know that the amount of V-Bucks you have available to you is displayed in the top right corner of the main menu in the small rectangular box that has a plus sign next to it. You can click on the plus sign if you want to buy more V-Bucks.

"So why would people spend money on something that doesn't give them a special ability in the game?" you may ask. The answer is that players who don't have cool cosmetics and a way to distinguish themselves from all the other players in the game don't feel unique. They feel like any other player with the boring default skin. Also, as mentioned in Chapter 9, the Battle Pass, which costs 950 V-Bucks, or $9.50, allows players to be rewarded with cosmetic items for playing the game and completing challenges. This may be another reason for buying V-Bucks: to buy a Battle Pass.

It's important to know that every item in the item shop has a rarity just like the in-game weapons that you pick up when looting. Accordingly, cosmetic items that are more rare will cost more V-Bucks. Whether or not the item is worth that much money is entirely the buyer's choice. Below is a chart of how many V-Bucks each item of each rarity costs.

Note: Currently there are no legendary pickaxes or legendary emotes in the game so it's impossible to know how much they would cost.

Item Pricing (V-Bucks)	Outfit	Pickaxe	Glider	Emote
LEGENDARY	2,000	None	2,000	None
EPIC	1,500	1,200	1,200	800
RARE	1,200	800	800	500
UNCOMMON	800	500	500	200
COMMON	None	None	None	None

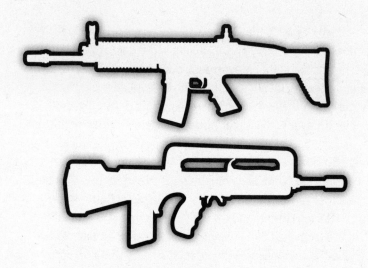

Banners

In Fortnite, you can unlock different icons by leveling up your account each season. You're given a set of colors to create unique banners to represent yourself. However, if you want more—often rare—icons for banners, you need to get your hands on the Battle Pass each season as there are typically quite a few icons available. You can earn your way through Battle Pass tiers by playing more games, which will unlock these exclusive icons for use on your banner.

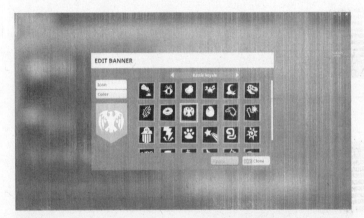

⏏ **This is the menu where you can edit your banner. You can choose to change your icon or your color. You can unlock more banner icons by leveling up your Battle Pass every season.**

The banner you create to represent you can be seen by others in the lobby tab next to your name before you start a game and to the left of your name at the top of the screen overlaying the shield. The banner is a customizable emblem that also shows your account level within the season, which your lost squadmates or decimated opponents can see after they're out of the game. Some players may argue that the banners on Fortnite are insignificant; however, other players would argue that banners are a cool though not terribly important way to showcase your creativity and differentiate yourself and your appearance. Banners can also be a cool way for you and your friends to establish an affiliation and play as a team or clan.

Outfits

Outfits in Fortnite Battle Royale go well beyond what characters are wearing. Outfits involve the characters' entire appearance: what they look like and what they wear is all determined by the outfit you choose. Through outfits, Epic Games is introducing new ways to differentiate yourself visually from other players on the battlefield. New outfits are being regularly introduced in the game.

⬆ The Tricera Ops outfit is currently the newest cosmetic outfit in the game. Almost every outfit comes with its own back bling as well. This outfit has a legendary rarity, which means it will cost more than other outfits that are of lower tiered rarity.

Why are different outfits so important? In squad situations, different outfit colors can help you distinguish comrades from enemies. Why would this be useful? If your teammate takes a player down after you've called out a player wearing a different outfit, this is an indication that the original player you called out is still alive and that your team should stay on alert. Your teammate runs the risk of pushing into a death trap as he believes, based on your call-out, that there was only one enemy who has now been eliminated when in reality there are multiple enemies.

Identifying outfits in solo games is extremely useful, too. For example, as you are gliding into the game early on, you can take note of the specific outfits worn by the people who are landing near you. Now that you have a decent idea of what is out there, based on different outfit colors, you know you won't feel entirely safe until you have accounted for all those people.

The outfits in Fortnite allow you to comfortably and easily customize your appearance to better portray yourself on the battlefield. The only real negative is that you can more easily be identified by opponents who will remember your outfit and search for you, but the reverse is also true, so you'll have to decide for yourself if this is actually a negative. Imagine how cool it would look to lead a full squad running around in the same skin.

You can acquire these different skinned outfits in the item shop in Fortnite using a variety of currency. You can use V-Bucks, earn your way through Battle Pass tiers or special events, or sometimes simply level up your account each season.

Back Bling

Back bling is a relatively new feature that essentially allows you to take what you are wearing on your back with specific outfits and match it with other outfits. Back bling generally comes with other skins, but there are exceptions in which back bling has been released specifically as stand-alone items in the item shop. The ability to mismatch back bling and outfits introduces more ways to make your character on the battlefield unique.

⬣ The Hatchling back bling is obtainable only by buying the Tricera Ops outfit from the item store.

Although back bling is typically small and usually cannot be identified as a defining visual trait from a distance, there are some instances in combat where back bling may give away your location. Some current back bling options extrude quite a bit from the character. This means back bling may be seen over, or around, your cover, revealing your location to the enemy. To avoid this, simply be sure to position your player carefully in situations where you intend to be stealthy. Also, keep an eye out for your enemy's bling; that negative can swiftly become a positive if the tables are turned and you are the one to notice back bling poking out behind cover.

Back bling can also be a cool way for you and your friends to establish association by wearing the same back bling with different skins, so you look different but still show relation to each other.

Harvesting Tools (Pickaxe)

Harvesting tools in Fortnite Battle Royale are very important. With harvesting tools you are able to obtain resources to potentially build your way out of any life-or-death situation. Who says you can't do this in style, however? Fortnite has released cosmetically appealing harvesting tool skins. From the default pickaxes to the Grim Reaper's scythe, there are many different harvesting tools to choose from.

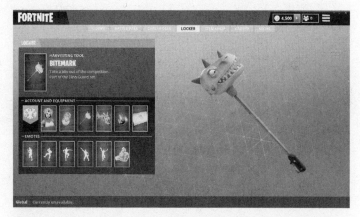

⏏ Harvesting tools and pickaxes are the same exact thing. It's confusing for some players to remember this, and it isn't uncommon for players to get confused when asked to hit down a tree with their harvesting tool. For the most part, stick to calling these items your pickaxe. It makes everything easier.

The harvesting tool skins in Fortnite can be earned through your Battle Pass tiers, by purchasing them from the item shop with V-Bucks, or sometimes by simply leveling up each season. Keep in mind that all the harvesting tools you can get make a unique sound when swung. Be sure to choose your harvesting tool based on both looks and the sound it makes. The sound should be a factor in your selection, because you can potentially give yourself away when farming for materials since some of the sounds are more noticeable than others.

Contrails

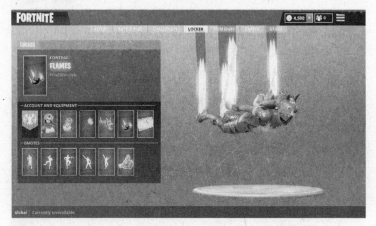

⊘ So far, contrails are obtainable only by completing Battle Pass challenges. The flames contrail was able to be obtained by reaching Battle Pass tier 84 in season 3.

Contrails, or skydiving trails, are new to the game and offer an interesting, though short-term way to customize your appearance and experience in the game. Contrails allow you to free-fall in style until you pull out your glider to finish landing. There are different patterns available so far, ranging from rainbows to fire that forms a streak behind you as you plummet toward the map. This feature can also be seen when using a launch pad and not pulling your glider out right away.

You can obtain contrails by leveling up your Battle Pass. However, as more contrails become available, they will be released in the item shop. There is also the possibility that in future seasons contrails will be available to earn from just leveling up your account during that season.

Be mindful that one downside of contrails is that they do help others see you as you land. Be conscious of your surroundings as you land in order to reduce this disadvantage, especially if your contrail is excessive, like the fire contrail available from season 3. Also, keep an eye out for other contrails; they will help you identify enemies around you at the start of the game.

Gliders

Gliders are tools used in the game to prevent you from dying when skydiving towards the ground. They can only be used at the start of the game when leaving the Battle Bus and when using a launch pad. As of season 3, you can only acquire glider skins by progressing through your Battle Pass tiers or purchasing them from the item shop with V-Bucks. As more gliders are released, there is a very real possibility that they will become available to those who simply level up during the season.

⌃ Once you reach a certain distance from the ground when skydiving, your player will automatically pull out a glider from a pocket. Gliders come in all sorts of wacky sizes, from an umbrella to a fire-breathing dragon. The High Octane glider was obtained by completing a certain set of challenges only available to players who reached tier 100 of their season 3 Battle Pass.

Some of the gliders in Fortnite can be quite visible; be sure to keep that in mind as you are playing. The larger your glider, the higher the probability that enemies can identify you in their vicinity at the start of the game. Look around as you land to spot other gliders, too.

Loading Screens

Loading screens are relatively new as of season 3 and are available only by passing through Battle Pass tiers. They are, quite simply, screens you get to choose to see while your game is loading.

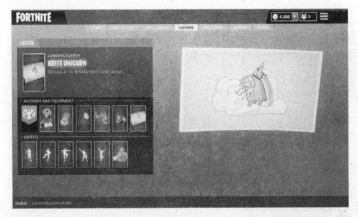

⬆ When transferring from the main menu to the pregame lobby, you will need to wait until a loading screen appears on your monitor. Unlike most other games, Fortnite allows you to customize this screen. Different loading screens can be obtained by completing tiers of the Battle Pass.

It's a fairly simple addition to the game, but it allows for more customization of the game, which most players appreciate. It's very likely loading screens will be available through the item shop, where you can buy them with V-Bucks.

Emotes

Emotes, which are taunts, take the crown in the realm of in-game celebration. You can select up to six emotes to be used to mess around with teammates, taunt enemies with the accompanying audio effects, and even disgrace opponents after you have reigned superior in battle by celebrating over their body with an anthem. There are many different emotes so far, from a simple clap to making it rain, with some retro music to set the mood.

A lot of other videogames have emotes. They are often used in a game to taunt players you are surrounded by, friend or foe. This one, called "Take the L," allows players to dance while holding up their hand to their forehead and making an L, signifying that another player is a loser. Emotes are all in good fun and should be treated as such; the other player may not *actually* be a loser—you may just be better at the game and want to gloat.

Emotes are available in the item shop, by grinding through tiers of your Battle Pass, and, in some instances, by simply leveling up during the season. Be careful when using emotes because they do tend to give away your position to nearby enemies. If opponents are walking by you while you're using certain emotes, they will hear you and become aware of your location, while you may be totally oblivious of them. Of course, emotes can also alert you to other players' positions, too, so you should investigate whenever you hear something that you suspect may be an emote.

Cosmetics serve a variety of uses. They provide no extra advantage to the player wearing them in-game, though sometimes they can be a disadvantage when playing with a group of friends. It is your job, as the player, to decide whether or not a cosmetic item is worth the money you would need to pay for it. There is no shortage of interesting new characters and add-on items you can use to customize your game.

CHAPTER 11

Basic Tips and Tricks

When players get into their first game of Fortnite, they are often overwhelmed by the amount of skill required to stay alive. For beginners, trying to figure out how to consistently get kills and get high placements is extremely hard. It's clear, once they've played two or three games, that Fortnite is a game unlike any other; that's what makes it so addicting.

To succeed at any game, players always look for ways to improve their playing style in order to increase their skill and efficiency. To shorten your learning curve and help you catch up to the rest of the Fortnite community, here are some basic tips and tricks to add to your game.

I. Always Have Building Materials

Having resources in Fortnite often makes the difference between life and death. That's because you can build your way out of just about any situation—as long as you have wood, metal, or brick at your disposal. If you fail to keep up with your wood, brick, and metal count, you may run out and lose the advantage of being able to defend yourself with walls, stairs, or floors.

When in need of healing, also use your building resources. Taking the time to build yourself a little panic fort after a fight has made you weak, or even during a fight when you need to subtract yourself for enough time to get some type of healing done, is always a good thing. Do not give your opponents the opportunity to catch you off-guard when you need to heal.

2. Build One-by-One Forts Often

⌂ Building one-by-one forts is an extremely effective way to shield yourself from other players who are trying to eliminate you. Building up multiple levels gives you the high ground and the advantage.

Building one-by-one forts either to get the high ground, to heal, or simply to hide is essential. Closing yourself in a box or building yourself a one-by-one tower will ensure that you always have a way to get to cover in a bad situation. These one-by-one structures are not the most sturdy, especially if made purely out of wood, but you can get your money's worth if players decide to take shots at your structure instead of at you. While they're focused on breaking down the wood, you can open fire on them from above.

Also, if enemies do go for your one-by-one structures, taking shots at your build reduces their ammo supply. If you can, take the time to replace the walls as they break from being shot out. This forces other players to waste more of their ammo shooting at your build until you are ready to strike back.

3. Play for the High Ground

Obtaining the high ground in Fortnite is one of the best advantages you can get. Either by building above people or taking shots at them from atop a higher elevation, such as mountains, plateaus, or buildings, you can be sure you see more of them than they do of you. However, be careful not to be head-shotted. Choose your shots wisely and take full advantage of the cover your high ground provides.

From the high ground, you not only have an advantage over the opponent you are engaging with, but, depending on the angles at work within your battleground, you can more easily spot people sneaking up on the altercation to take shots at you while you are weak from the fight you are in. Always take the time to get above your opponent's elevation when you can. It may mean the difference between life and death.

▲ Building yourself to a high elevation is key to winning every gunfight. Players below you can only see your head when you're shooting down at them, whereas you can see their entire body while you're crouching behind cover.

4. Build Two Stairs Wide When Attacking Other Players

When you are pushing opponents in a battle, be sure to build between you and the players you are facing. Simply building anything that obstructs their line of sight will be enough sometimes, but to truly seize the opportunity, you are going to want to build two stairs wide toward them. To do this, sprint up the middle of your two-stair-wide ramp, making it easier for you to place the next level. While the stairs are giving you a vertical advantage as you build higher and higher, each set of stairs will support the other set in the event your opponents decide to take shots at the base of your stairs. Your opponents will thus need more shots to take down your structure, giving you more time to become aware that they are destroying your build. Finally, when you come face-to-face with them, they will have less ammo, whereas you will have a full magazine to fight with.

⬆ By rushing your opponents while building two stairs at a time, you force them to have to shoot out two ramps instead of one, while you quickly gain the height advantage and close the gap between yourself and your enemies.

5. Adjust Your Settings to What Is Most Comfortable to You

Adjusting your settings in the game can boost your performance in many ways. Especially if you are using a PC, adjusting the way you are playing through in-game options can affect your overall performance. For example, lowering your texture or shadow settings can increase the frames per second you experience in the game, thus boosting your overall awareness and responsiveness in most situations. Even adjusting the brightness of your screen helps. At some points your game can be blinding if you do not adjust the brightness, and at other times you can't see what's in front of you.

Also in your settings are the controller and input options. As with most games, you will probably be satisfied with Fortnite's default settings at first, but you may come to realize that you would rather be able to perform some actions by pressing different buttons. For PC users, the default building keybinds are F1 through F5, which are extremely awkward to use in almost any situation. Many players assign these building input settings to different keys for ease of access, so they don't have to stretch their hand across their keyboard in order to complete a basic, even necessary, task. Instead of using F1 through F5, players often bind their walls to the Z key, floors to the X key, and ramps to the F or C keys. Adjusting which action goes to which key is entirely up to you, so you should consider carefully what adjustments would make each action as effortless as possible.

6. Get a Mouse With Side Buttons

For PC users, getting a lightweight mouse with buttons on the side will give you a clear advantage over your opponents. Building is the skill that will make or break you in Fortnite, and building by pressing multiple buttons on your keyboard can be confusing and certainly inefficient. However, with a mouse, such as the Razer: Mamba or Finalmouse Ultralight Pro, which are two of the best mice on the market right now, you can use the two buttons on the left-hand side to switch to your walls or ramps instantly. This is extremely helpful in tense situations when other players panic and can't find the right buttons on their keyboard, but you only have to hit one or two mouse buttons with your thumb.

7. Watch Fortnite Streamers

Watching other players, especially those who are ranked among the best by their peers, can be a great way to study the art of being a champion. You can watch videos featuring good players, but you'll learn more by watching top players on stream. The best website to do this on is www.twitch.tv.

Seeing good players live and being able to interact with them or ask questions within their chat can help you understand what you are doing wrong and learn how to get better at the game. Watching people when they are live also shows you examples of good players getting bad results. You may see even excellent players lose more often than they win. Not only should this put you at ease when you don't perform at your peak, but you can also see what they do wrong and apply that knowledge to your own gameplay. Watching the people who have the most viewers while streaming Fortnite, you can learn new techniques that you can then try out in your own games.

Watching Twitch streamers is also a good way to get involved in the community of Fortnite enthusiasts, which can, in some instances, help you find people to duo or squad up with in your pursuit of victory.

8. Learn Your Limitations

Understanding your limits in the game, such as how far you can fall without taking fall damage, is an extremely important thing to learn. When you are trying to evade an enemy and you need to know if a fall will kill you with low health, having that in-game sense that comes with experience will be very useful. When you are faced with a fall that you know is too great for you to come out of unharmed, build floors underneath you to cushion your fall as you descend.

Similarly, knowing how high you can jump on Fortnite will enable you to take full advantage of potential paths on an escape route or even in an assault against an enemy. Being mindful of your vertical capabilities can aid you in jumping over walls, getting off shots before you fall too low, and evaluating the risk in jumping from lower elevations to higher ones. Understanding your ability to jump is a must.

When you're in a fight, understanding how quickly you are losing health with each shot that your opponent lands is another very important thing to take note of. Realizing how weak you are becoming with each shot, you'll know when you will have to back off in order to heal before it is too late. This basic yet hard-to-master sense will give you a better chance of coming out on top in battle.

Fully understanding what you can and can't do with your inventory is also critical. You can only hold things within your inventory in up to five slots, with the exception of utilities and ammunition. This means you can only hold five weapons or means of healing. Be sure you understand which items are more valuable than others in order to maximize the usefulness of your inventory. This is not a rule that is set in stone; developing these personal preferences will require some experience. Be mindful of how many items you can hold in a stack within one slot of your inventory, and weigh out your options carefully. Utilizing your inventory to its full potential will aid you in your quest to become the best on the battlefield.

9. Play the Game

As in any game, task, or action in life, if you want to get good at something you have to do it often. The game of Fortnite is no exception. By far, the best way to get better at the game is to play as often as you can (so long as you have the time). If the game is something you decide you are passionate about and thus you want to get better at it, you need to be willing to dedicate the time it will take to achieve your goal. There are plenty of gamers out there who have racked up thousands of hours playing certain video games, and it isn't because they're losers with no social lives—it's because they've found something they're passionate about and they've stuck with it. This is the story of almost every single professional gamer you will ever see or hear of. Should you set your first goal to be a professional player? Probably not—but the goal of "Today I want to get three solo wins" is entirely possible and worth setting. As you get better at Fortnite, you should set new goals and learn to become your own critic in order to get them done and improve after every mistake.

CHAPTER 12

Advanced Tips and Tricks

Reaching the level of an advanced Fortnite player is no easy task. It requires dozens—even hundreds—of hours playing the game, learning the techniques, and building in order to confidently and consistently achieve Victory Royale in nearly every game you play. Advanced players all use computers because a mouse and keyboard give users more control versus playing with a controller. If you want to be one of the best Fortnite players, make sure you're playing on a PC. Once you're an advanced player, it's very difficult to improve your strategy significantly, but that doesn't mean it can't be done. There is always a way to do something better.

These advanced tips and tricks have been hard for even some of the best players to learn, let alone master. But they will certainly improve your gameplay.

I. Use Impulse Grenades

One of the best additions to Fortnite was the new weapon called the impulse grenade. This grenade does no actual damage to any of the players hit by its explosion, but if it explodes near you it will send you flying away from it. This unique item has brought all sorts of new strategies into the game. For example, players can move to attack a distant enemy by running forward, throwing the grenade on the ground, and jumping, a move that sends them flying toward their opponent.

You don't always have to use impulse grenades in situations with opponents, though. Impulse grenades will also allow you a little bit of extra time while you're running away from the incoming storm. If you simply run forward, look straight down at the ground, throw the impulse grenade while running, and jump, your player will be sent flying forward without taking any fall damage. This method works on any flat surface in the game and can be used in all kinds of creative ways.

2. Place Walls in Front of Your Ramps

In addition to building your double ramps (as mentioned in Chapter 11), another way to strike fear into your opponent is to place walls in front of your ramps so that it is even more difficult for enemies to shoot out the platforms you've built to gain the high ground. You'll have a clear advantage. By practicing this technique often and mastering it, you will send a clear message to all who encounter you that you are the better player.

⏶ Putting walls in front of your ramps adds an extra layer of protection to your ramps, making it harder for enemy players to destroy them.

3. Outplay Players Who Have the High Ground on You

With all this talk of winning by gaining the high ground, you may still often struggle when your opponent has the high ground and you are left below. Nothing is more frustrating than using ramps to rush toward an opponent only to have your enemy place a structure over you while quickly rising above you and building a fort. So what do you do?

⬆ Imagine that you and an opponent have rushed straight toward each other and that your opponent gained the high ground and built a small fort above you to use to shoot down on you. This is what your situation would look like.

There are two very similar ways to regain the high ground from an opponent who has a height advantage over you. You need to "reset" yourself by building around the fort blocking your path and then building up in order to shoot down on the enemy.

The first strategy is to build ramps around the fort your opponent put in your way so you can attack from behind. This method only works in some situations but can be extremely effective when used properly. Most enemy players are too focused on their own builds to pay attention to what you may be doing while they panic. However, some very good players will see this coming and box themselves into their own one-by-one fort as a result. If they do this, use ramps to build up the sides of their new tower and beat them to the top.

⬦ **This picture shows what your path would look like if you built ramps in order to climb around the side of an opponent's fort that was right above you. By using ramps to build along the side of the fort, you can keep your momentum while attacking the enemy.**

The second and more reliable method of countering an opponent who has the high ground is to turn around and build two floors and then some ramps in order to get around whatever may be in your way. Using floors as an alternative is extremely useful if you need to turn around and get out from under the enemy's fort and also build your way above it.

 This image shows a variation of the ramp technique. This method of gaining the high ground allows you to use floors to escape from underneath the enemy fort. Using floors is a smarter play because you lose slightly less height while beginning to build up a pathway so that you can shoot down on the enemy.

Lastly, imagine another situation where you are directly underneath an enemy. While you hide in your panic fort, edit an opening into your wall and then use ramps to build up from the side of your box. When using this method, you must also place ramps above you in order to shield yourself from the opponent who would otherwise be able to shoot you in the back. Once you've built a few ramps away from your panic fort, build one extra ramp on the bottom, turn around 180 degrees, place a floor beneath you, and finally build one more ramp with a wall in front of it so that you can shoot back down onto your opponent.

Step 1 in performing the technique of using ramps to gain a height advantage on an opponent directly above you is to block yourself off from any outside openings and enclose yourself in a box. Step 2 is to edit an opening in one of the walls of your box and use your ramps to create an incline for you to run on as well as a shield to protect you from the enemy on the roof of your fort.

The third and final step is to place an extra ramp in front of you, turn around 180 degrees, place a floor beneath you, and then build a ramp with a wall in order to give yourself some extra cover while you shoot down at your enemy.

4. Replace Enemy Structures With Your Own

There may be times when you have the high ground over opponents beneath you, but they have blocked themselves off in their own fort so they can heal themselves while you attempt to break through their walls. Nine out of ten times, players in your position will simply shoot out the wall while standing right above it, only to see your opponent keep quickly rebuilding the wall until you run out of ammo to shoot it with. Here's the solution: Don't shoot the wall.

Instead, use your pickaxe to smash the wall down and then quickly place your own wall where your opponent's old one once stood. Doing this may seem counterproductive as there is still a wall between you and your opponent, but now *you* have the ability to edit the wall. So you can, for example, place a window in it. Now, while your opponent is cornered in the base, you simply shoot into the box or maybe throw grenades. Either way, using this technique will give you the upper hand and force your opponent to quickly react to your intelligent play, which may be impossible.

5. Use Edit Mode to See Through Walls

In order to edit structures in the game, you select tiles of walls or floors that you want to disappear or change. When you go into editing mode, the structure you wish to edit gets divided into blue squares. When you click on these blue squares, they disappear and you can see through the object you are editing while still staying safe.

This editing exploit provides a unique strategy that you can use in tense situations. By editing a structure and selecting tiles to disappear but then not confirming the edit, you can see your surroundings through the structure while all other players are left clueless. It's like x-ray vision.

One way of using this strategy is toward the end of a game when there are very few players left to eliminate, but you need to heal yourself before attacking them. After you've finished healing yourself in a one-by-one fort, you can select a wall to edit, then select all the tiles, and thus gather information about what is happening around you without exposing yourself to your opponents.

By using the edit mode to select all the tiles of a wall, you will be able to see through the wall while it still keeps you safe. Using this technique can provide you with a large amount of useful information without putting yourself in danger.

6. Stay Confident

This tip may seem a bit redundant and unhelpful at first, but depending on the way you tackle the game, confidence could be what aids you the most on your quest to become the best in the lobby. The most important thing to do in Fortnite when putting all your newly found knowledge to the test is to remain confident. If you play with confidence, even if it gets you killed in your first few games, you will end up being the one who unconditionally applies pressure. This means you will be relentless. Your knowledge of how the game works will allow you to force your opponents into danger and they won't have any way to counter you.

Being confident in Fortnite isn't about pushing when you shouldn't; being confident is about seizing every opportunity in which you know you have the upper hand. Be sure that you always apply all your new knowledge of the game, affecting every decision you make. Take the time to think about how your engagements might pan out. In other words, imagine every move your opponents can make to best you, and try your hardest to be prepared for each possibility. Have a Plan A, B, and C, not just Plan A. Focus on what your enemies can do to build out of the situation and how you can maintain the high ground. There are many variables to keep in mind, and as the confident aggressor, you need to evaluate each situation.

Taking the time to learn these tips, even if it takes a while to master them, will make you a force to be reckoned with in the game. Everything that goes into your play-by-play decision-making needs to be about how to best take advantage of your present situation. Reading your environment and adjusting the way you play to the circumstances of particular fights are the most important things to know how to do in this game. Do not expect to be able to do the same thing in every fight just because it works one time. Always switch up the way you tackle every situation. Fully utilizing these tips will provide an advantage within your games that most people in the lobby will not be able to match.

CHAPTER 13

Playback Feature

One of the game's most useful tools for improving your skills in Fortnite is the playback feature, which you can use to watch your past game-plays. Sometimes when you get eliminated, it's not quite clear what mistake you made that allowed your opponent to knock you out of the game. However, by using the playback feature you can watch the game from any player's perspective and even through the eye of a free-roam camera, in order to get a better view of what you could have done to improve your arsenal of techniques.

If you would like to go back and look over what happened in a game, whether you won or lost, go to the Career tab on the main menu and select the Replays option.

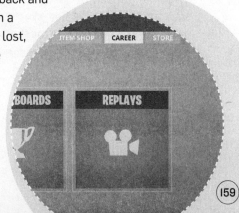

▲ The Career tab is along the top bar of the main menu. Here, you can view some of your stats as well as some of your friends' stats through the Profile and Leaderboards options.

▲ Upon selecting the Replays option, you will see a list of all your previous games. The most recent games will be at the top of the list and the oldest games will be at the bottom.

Once you have found the game you wish to look back at, select it and then click the Play button in the bottom right corner of the screen. After a short loading screen, the replay will start from the very moment you entered the lobby even before the game actually started. You will see a timeline bar along the bottom of the screen with a bunch of marks that indicate when you got kills and when you got headshots hovering over it, as well as the play and rewind options underneath.

Fortnite's playback feature has several special options that often go overlooked and unused. The most useful is the camera perspective option. To get to this, click on the camera button at the far right under the timeline bar. The current mode selected is often "Third Person"; however, that is not the only camera perspective you have to watch the playback from.

To the left of the camera perspective option button is the name of the player you are currently watching. You are not limited to watching only your own perspective of the game, but if you are unsure about which person you are spectating, scroll to the left or to the right until your username appears in that box. To watch someone else, select the name from the list of players in the lobby, which can be found by clicking the second button from the left edge of the screen.

The perspectives of the player you can use to watch your replay are Drone Free, Drone Attach, Drone Follow, Gameplay, and Third Person. Drone Free allows you to view the game from any angle, like a drone. Drone Attach means that the drone's position changes every time the player it is watching moves. If the player goes forward, the drone goes forward. However, this particular setting does not change the angle of the drone's view. While in this mode, the drone can still look left and right; it is not centered on the player. The Drone Follow option is the opposite of the Drone Attach option. When the player moves, the drone does not, and the camera is fixed on watching the player. The Gameplay setting allows you to watch your replay from the exact same perspective that you had when you were originally playing. Lastly, the Third Person option can operate halfway between the Drone Attach and Drone Follow options. The camera is always focused on the player, following the player around. However, you can move the camera around as if it had a string tied to the character straight from the lens.

If you really enjoy photography, the playback feature has even more options that you will love. By selecting the button that depicts a camera with a gear in it, to the left of the rewind arrows, you will be able to tweak a variety of camera settings.

⬣ **Using the Third Person camera option, you can experiment with these settings in order to get high-quality images and perspectives for purposes like making YouTube videos and montages.**

In April 2018, Epic Games held a competition called the Replay Royale Contest in order to celebrate the launch of Fortnite's playback feature. Epic Games understands that a lot can be done with a polished and user-friendly replay mode. Thus, the company challenged players to use the new feature in order to make a 60- to 90-second-long video that showed a mastery of the new system as well as a unique and creative representation of the game.

◢ **On April 13, 2018, Epic Games announced its Replay Royale Contest, which gave anyone the opportunity to win a brand-new gaming computer, a 30-minute conference call with the Epic Games Video Team, a Fortnite "Swag Bag," and 10,000 V-Bucks.**

At the end of the competition, the winners were announced on the Epic Games website. A user by the name of "Enzait" won the competition with a submission titled "Revenge."

REVENGE

REVENGE · A Fortnite Cinematic #ReplayRoyale

428,655 views

Published on Apr 23, 2018
Revenge is Sweet

"Revenge" is a very action-packed Fortnite cinematic video that tells a humorous story about a player's journey to hunt down an opponent who called him a loser in the pregame lobby of a Fortnite match.

If you're not into cinematography and video editing, you can still use some additional options of Fortnite's playback feature that serve its original purpose by making it easy to see where players were, what weapons they had, how much health they had, and even how much damage they took from each hit.

By watching your playback, you can critique your building habits, your shooting habits, and the way you play the game as a whole. Maybe you built the wrong way or didn't put walls in front of your ramps, leaving your structures vulnerable. It's also possible that you died because you peeked your head above your base for too long and got sniped, so you should remember to take cover more often. Criticizing your own gameplay and reflecting on your decisions are extremely helpful in improving your skills.

⬆ Professional teams often use the playback feature to take notes on how they lost a game in a competition or tournament so that they can learn how to prevent such a loss from happening again.

Glossary

airdrop Like chests, airdrops are containers full of loot; however, they fall from the sky randomly during the game.

ammunition Ammunition is fired from various weapons in Fortnite to inflict damage upon opponents.

back bling An element of customization that allows you to change the item on your character's back. Back bling typically comes with outfits that can be bought in the item shop.

bandage Bandages are a resource used to replenish your health until you hit 75 percent. Once you reach that point, you can no longer use bandages to heal and will need to resort to alternatives to reach full health.

Battle Bus The means of transportation at a high altitude before you drop to land. The Battle Bus follows a straight line in one particular direction across the map.

Battle Pass A feature that grants players rewards in exchange for leveling up within the game. A Battle Pass costs 950 V-Bucks or $9.50 USD.

Battle Royale A type of game in which individual players, or teams, compete against their opponents within one playing area that shrinks as time progresses.

bloom The crosshair displays the area you are aiming at, but your bullets may not go perfectly straight, thus adding a random element to the game. This effect is known as bloom.

bolt action Bolt action is a type of firearm action in which cartridges are moved into and out of the weapon's barrel chamber when the shooter manually manipulates the bolt directly via a handle.

boogie bomb A grenade-like item that can be thrown at enemy players in order to make them dance for a short period of time or until they receive damage.

building The act of assembling structures on the island, typically in a strategic manner.

burst assault rifle The burst assault rifle fires three bullets every time you shoot. Only the first bullet will be 100 percent accurate, whereas the other two will be random.

chest Chests are lootable containers spawned throughout the map that contain potential weapons, healing supplies, ammunition, and utilities.

chug jug An item that restores a player's health and shield each to 100 percent. A chug jug takes 15 seconds to consume.

contrail A customizable effect that follows your character as you skydive to the surface of the island at the beginning of each game.

cozy campfire An item that heals players who stand around it for a brief time.

crosshair The crosshair is a HUD display, or a feature of a scoped weapon, that visually conveys where your shots will or may land.

damage Damage points counter health points; as your enemies cause damage to you, your health points diminish.

edit mode The ability to reconfigure structures placed by you or your squadmates in Fortnite.

emote Action you can make your character perform in a theatrical manner that can help communicate with teammates and other players.

Epic Games The game development company that created, and thus owns, the title Fortnite.

experience points Points given to players upon completion of each game of Fortnite Battle Royale. Gaining experience allows players to ascend to the next level of the game, but not to the next tier of their Battle Pass.

glider Fortnite's version of a parachute. A glider is a device that is used at the beginning of each game when a player skydives toward the ground.

grenade An explosive device that can be thrown at other players.

gunfight Any battle in which weapons are fired.

hand cannon A high-caliber pistol.

health Health refers to how much damage you can sustain before being downed or killed. Your health is represented by a 100-point system; each time you are hurt, you lose a fraction of those points.

height advantage You gain a height advantage in battle when you are at a higher altitude than your opponents.

high ground Any point on the map in Fortnite that is at a higher elevation than the surrounding area.

hop rocks Consumable items that can be found throughout the map in meteor divots. They allow players to experience low gravity.

HUD The HUD, or heads-up display, is any transparent display that presents data without requiring users to look away from their usual viewpoints. This includes the health and shield bars, the mini-map, the compass, and all the weapon slots and building slots in the bottom right corner of the screen.

impulse grenade An explosive weapon in Battle Royale. It can be thrown to launch enemies and the players themselves away from the point of impact.

item shop A tab on the main menu of Fortnite that offers plenty of daily and featured cosmetic items. Buying items from the item shop only changes your character's appearance; it does not grant any in-game advantage.

launch pad A legendary item that allows players to travel far distances by launching them in the air and allowing them to glide to the ground.

levels Players ascend through levels by playing games of Fortnite Battle Royale and performing well. Do not confuse levels with the tiers of the Battle Pass.

light machine gun The light machine gun works similar to the minigun with its high fire rate and high damage to enemy structures; however, it can only fire 100 bullets per magazine.

llama piñata Llama piñatas spawn randomly and extremely rarely in Fortnite. They are loot containers that have healing supplies, ammunition, and, most notably, materials. Each llama piñata contains 500 resources of each material type, totaling 1,500 materials.

loot Anything that can be picked up and/or consumed during the game.

magazine A device used to house bullets that can be inserted into weapons in order to maximize efficiency.

material Materials are used to build structures on Fortnite.

med kit Med kits are a resource used to fully replenish health.

minigun A six-barrel rotary machine gun with a high rate of fire (2,000 to 6,000 rounds per minute); it can also fire at a high sustained rate.

mini-map The mini-map is a tool located on the HUD that identifies your location on the map and allows you to see the safe zone and the direction to take to reach it.

outfit Your character's main appearance that can be customized in the locker.

panic fort When you are caught off guard in a battle, you can build a panic fort as a quick defensive maneuver to avoid taking damage.

PC A personal computer.

pickaxe A pickaxe is a tool in Fortnite used to harvest materials from objects.

PlayerUnknown's Battlegrounds A rival game to Fortnite Battle Royale within the Battle Royale genre.

PlayStation 4 A gaming console created by Sony that players can use to play a vast variety of video games, including Fortnite.

PlayStation Plus The membership players must have on their PlayStation Network account in order to play online games with their friends. A membership costs $9.99 per month.

port-a-fort A device that sprouts a small metal fort when thrown at the ground.

pump shotgun A type of shotgun that fires slowly but increases accuracy and damage as a result.

rarity The likelihood that a weapon or other item will be found during the game. Items with low rarity are very common and less powerful. Items that are rarer are less common and more powerful.

recoil When you fire any weapon in Fortnite, the gun will pop up as a reaction to the bullets being fired. This is known as recoil.

remote explosives Explosive devices that can be stuck to walls and then detonated all at once.

revolver A type of pistol that holds six high-caliber bullets in its revolving chamber at a time.

safe zone An area of safety on the map which shrinks throughout the game. In each game the safe zone appears randomly.

SCAR A popular assault rifle in modern video games. It serves as a deadly weapon in Fortnite Battle Royale. SCAR stands for Special Operations Combat Assault Rifle.

season The time players have to complete all the tiers of a Battle Pass. Each season has new rewards in each tier.

semiautomatic assault rifle The semiautomatic assault rifle uses medium ammunition to fire rounds at medium- to long-range opponents.

shield A means of providing protection for your character.

shipping container Structure made of metal designed to hold objects. Open shipping containers can sometimes contain chests.

slurp juice A consumable item that grants 25 health points and 25 shield points over a short duration of time.

sniper rifle A weapon that is able to fire at extremely long ranges with high accuracy. Snipers often use a magnified scope in order to allow the user to aim at a target from far distances.

spawning Spawning refers to the initial appearance of characters in the game or items on the map. For example, players first spawn on the Battle Bus; chests spawn on the island.

stars Rewarded for completing challenges and leveling up, stars allow players to progress through their Battle Pass. Ten stars are needed to pass through each tier of the Battle Pass.

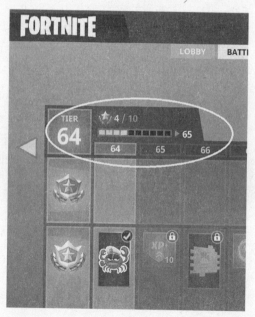

storm The storm surrounds the safe zone and inflicts damage upon those those who remain outside it. To preserve their health, players should avoid the storm at all costs.

structure A generic term for one of the things a player can build with the building feature in the game.

suppressed submachine gun The suppressed submachine gun uses light ammunition to quickly fire several low-damage rounds at close-range opponents.

tactical shotgun A type of shotgun that fires quickly at the expense of accuracy and damage.

tiers The ranks of the Battle Pass that players can progress through, earning rewards for their completion.

V-Bucks In-game currency that can be received by ranking up a Battle Pass or by buying with real-world currency. V-Bucks are used to buy tiers of the Battle Pass and to purchase items in the item shop.

vending machine Vending machines on Fortnite allow you to purchase weapons in exchange for building materials already in your possession. Each vending machine contains items of one rarity. Depending on the rarity of an item, the more materials it will cost.

Victory Royale Also called a "win," this is what is displayed on a banner across the screen of a player who has won a game of Fortnite Battle Royale at the end of the match.

Xbox Live Like PlayStation Plus, this is a membership service that allows players to play online multiplayer games with their friends. The membership costs $9.99 per month.

Xbox One A gaming console created by Microsoft that players can use to play Fortnite. Xbox One and PlayStation 4 are both similar and different in many ways.

Resources

When people play Fortnite, they play in order to get better at the game. The competitive aspect of the game is what keeps players coming back time and time again. In order to be the best at anything, you have to devote time and effort to fixing your mistakes and learning how to perform better than everyone else. While everyone learns at different rates, playing the game is the best way to improve your skills and figure out the best approaches to beating your opponents. However, there are some shortcuts that can save you hours of playing time—you still have to play, but these resources can help you figure out where to focus your attention and what strategies are most effective. They even allow you to watch over the shoulders of some of the best Fortnite players out there.

The following are places you can turn to for more instruction. By visiting these resources, including players to watch, websites, and videos, you will be able to increase your knowledge about the game exponentially. Some of the resources even have other resources you can visit within them.

#1 Victory Royale!

WEBSITES

Epic Games
www.epicgames.com

Epic Games is the development studio that created Fortnite and has a reputation for being one of the most transparent developers in the gaming industry. If you ever want to catch up on Fortnite news or investigate a rumor, the most reliable source is the developers of the game themselves. The website is extremely user-friendly, filled with easy-to-use features and a lot of eye candy.

⌃ On the Epic Games website you can log into your account and link all your Fortnite accounts. That is, you can link your PC to your Xbox Live, mobile, or PlayStation Plus account so that you can play on any platform.

Besides making it easy for you to handle your account, the Epic Games website is also where you can stay on top of the latest news about the game. In May 2018, Epic Games announced on its website that the company will establish prize pools worth a total of $100 million for competitive Fortnite tournaments in 2018 and 2019. This is, by a huge margin, the largest amount of money any game developer has dedicated to help fund the competitive aspect of its own game.

Check back at the website to find out about upcoming tournaments.

Fortnite Chests Info
www.fortnitechests.info

Although this book includes the chest spots for all the
named landing locations as of season 4, week 3, the Fortnite
Chests website has every chest location on the Fortnite map
marked and updated. Besides getting an overhead view of
the island and the chest locations, you can interact with the
map by clicking on a chest icon and seeing a picture of the
chest and its surroundings in order to make finding each one
even easier.

⏺ **The home page of www.fortnitechests.info allows anyone
to find any chest just by clicking on the map on the left side of
the screen; no account is needed.**

This website has many useful features that aren't just chest
locations. Players can also find the locations of vending
machines and ammo crates, and there is even a page dedi-
cated to helping players complete their weekly Battle Pass
challenges so that they can earn rewards quicker.

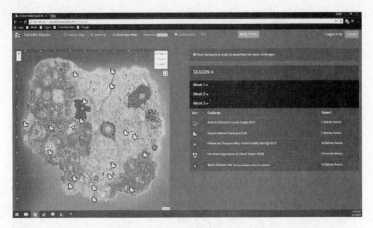

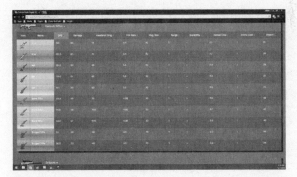

You can view the challenges not just for one week but for any combination of weeks by selecting which ones you'd like to see in the top right corner of the map. What the website calls "battle points" this book calls "stars."

One last feature this website offers is a chart showing all the statistics about the weapons in the game. It categorizes the weapons by range, rarity, amount of damage that they can deal per second, and other characteristics.

This extremely helpful data chart on the weapons page of fortnitechests.info shows players which weapons are the most appropriate in each situation.

Fortnite Master
www.fortnitemaster.com

If you are getting better at Fortnite and have a couple of wins, a site that provides a lot of statistics on your gameplay is fortnitemaster.com. Not only can you track your progress, you can also check out the progress of your friends and a boatload of popular names in the Fortnite community as well.

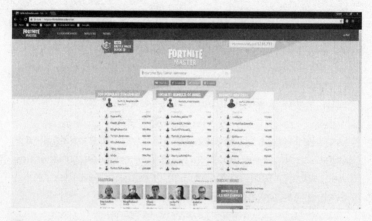

▲ If you play Fortnite on a PC, all you have to do in order to get your statistics is enter your Epic Games username. If you play on a console, then you will have to go to epicgames.com and link your PlayStation Plus or Xbox Live account to your Epic Games account before you can use this resource.

Fortnite Issues Trello
https://trello.com/b/Bs7hgkma /fortnite-community-issues

Have you ever played a video game that had a bunch of glitches and problems that needed to be fixed by the game developers? Chances are that you have, whether you know it or not. No video game is perfect from the start; because of the complexity of games today, there are often glitches or "bugs" that end up in the game as a result of erroneous coding. This Trello website is Epic Games' official community bug page that lets players know whether or not a bug has been found, has been fixed, or will be fixed within the next game update. This is an extremely helpful resource because every once in a while a bug will be the reason you get eliminated in any video game, and that's frustrating. However, knowing that the reason your character died was the game's fault, not yours, can save you a lot of frustration and give you the hope you need to keep playing and improving.

⬣ After every game update, this website is edited by the developers of Fortnite in order to keep the community up to date and provide transparency.

Fortnite Battle Royal Reddit
www.reddit.com/r/fortnitebr

Often referred to as the front page of the Internet, Reddit is well known for being a single place where an entire community can come together. Through the creation of what is called a subreddit, the Fortnite Battle Royale community has become one of the largest on the website with just under 630,000 subscribers. If you want to stay up to date on all things Fortnite—strategies, suggestions, bugs, and more—this forum is the place to go.

◆ When you visit the Fortnite Battle Royale subreddit, this is the first page you will see. If you see a topic you want to learn more about (for example, Mentor Monday), just click on the title.

PEOPLE TO WATCH

Ninja
www.twitch.tv/ninja

"Ninja" is one of the most popular Internet figures as of the writing of this book, and for good reason. By playing Fortnite for his viewers live on a platform called Twitch, Ninja has quickly risen to become one of the most well-known icons online. Twitch is a great platform that allows people to watch and interact with their favorite figures. It's extremely difficult to be successful as a Twitch streamer because you have to be entertaining 100 percent of the time you are live, usually for hours on end, but Ninja manages to do it.

⬆ **Ninja is one of the best Fortnite players. Just by watching him play and mimicking his playstyle, you will be able to improve your skills as a result.**

Myth
www.twitch.tv/tsm_myth

A player using the alias Myth, who plays competitive Fortnite for his organization Team Solomid (TSM), was given the nickname "The Young Architect" because of his extremely fast and calculated building skills in Fortnite. By watching Myth, many players hope to improve their building skills, learn new tricks to get out of tight situations, or just relax and watch an entertaining Twitch stream.

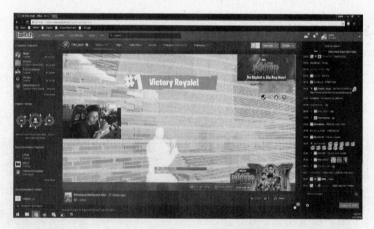

Myth wins his first game of the day in the Solo Showdown limited-time game mode. If he is not live, anyone can go back and watch Myth's previous streams by going to his videos tab on his Twitch channel.

cLoakzy
www.twitch.tv/cloakzy

A professional Fortnite player for the organization FaZe Clan, cLoakzy offers an enjoyable and mature stream that never disappoints in providing unique ways to play Fortnite. In the small number of Fortnite tournaments that have taken place so far, cLoakzy and the rest of the FaZe roster have already demonstrated that they are a dominant force in the competitive Fortnite scene.

cLoakzy wins a solo game with 14 kills.

ABOUT THE AUTHOR

Grant Turner is an avid gamer and a student at the Rochester Institute of Technology. He's been playing video games for more than 10 years.

Fortnite is one of the games he plays regularly, and he estimates he has invested more than 150 hours in it. He also has about 500 hours in H1Z1, another battle royale game. He's played more than 700 hours on Counter Strike: Global Offensive and has spent many hours on Battalion 1944, Call of Duty, and Halo.

Unlike some gamers who play occasionally, Grant keeps up-to-date on the games, closely following the news about the companies that produce them and the industry as a whole.

Although not a professional competitor himself, he has attended Major League Gaming events in Columbus, Ohio, and Ultimate Gaming Challenge: Niagara twice.